ALSO BY JOHN B. "RED" CUMMINGS, JR.

*Lobstah Tales: A History of the Moby Dick/Back Eddy
Restaurant in Westport, Massachusetts* (2016)

Cream of the Crop: Fall River's Best and Brightest (2014)

*The Last Fling: Hurricane Carol 1954,
Stories from Westport, Massachusetts* (2011)

MURDER, MANSLAUGHTER, AND MAYHEM
ON THE SOUTHCOAST

VOLUME ONE 1800 TO 1969

JOHN B. "RED" CUMMINGS, JR.

WITH STEFANI KOOREY, PHD

Hillside Media

Westport, Massachusetts

Hillside Media
Westport, Massachusetts

All inquires should be sent to:
John B. Cummings Jr.
Hillside Media
245 Old Harbor Road
Westport, MA 02790
Tel: 508.636.2831
or John@hillsidemedia.net

ISBN-10: 154666226X
ISBN-13: 978-1546662266

Printed in the United States of America on acid-free paper.

Book and cover design by Stefani Koorey, PearTree Press, Fall River, MA

MURDER, MANSLAUGHTER, AND MAYHEM ON THE SOUTHCOAST

Dedication

To Law Enforcement

In recent months, law enforcement officials have been maligned. Their job could not be more difficult. They deserve our thanks and praise.

Both men and women willingly sign on to protect and serve the citizenry. On the following pages the reader will find mini biographies of those who have violated the law and those who have been murdered. Most have broken the law multiple times prior to the ultimate crime they were accused of committing. Their backgrounds of illegal activity are ofen missing but many were very familiar to local and, oftentimes, state law enforcement officials. We honor those law enforcement officials who investigated these cases, found the bad guys, and helped bring justice for the victims.

CONTENTS

PREFACE

Upon setting out to chronicle *Murder, Manslaughter, and Mayhem on the SouthCoast*, I wanted to call attention to the victims as well as the accused. I did not include motor vehicle homicides even though they are as devastating to the victim's families as are other types of deaths.

The story of the Borden murders is not only well known in the area but internationally as well. It did not need to be repeated here but this book would not be complete without it. There are many other cases that were just as horrific. The very first slaying in this book occurred, technically, in Tiverton, Rhode Island, and the near final one in 2016 (to be detailed in volume 2) also happened there. In the first, the pregnant 29-year-old working girl and the accused minister (and like the Borden murders, unsolved) generated a great deal of press and debate. Many others have as well. The context of these crimes is important to understand as the local culture and political environment also played roles in the events over the years—

Gray

Gray—even when it is sunny, it is gray in these old New England mill cities.

Gray because of the multi-family mill housing.

Gray because of the granite block four and five story massive mill buildings.

Gray because of the color of the cloth produced.

Gray because of the mill employees clothing.

Gray because of the lunch pails.

Gray because of the paved cobblestone streets.

Gray because of the axes and hatches.

Gray because of the pollution from the smoke stacks.

Gray because of the river pollution from the mills.

Gray because of the human depression and the helplessness of the mill workers who shopped at the mill stores, lived in the mill housing and were held back with mill wages.

Many of the slayings in this book remain unsolved and open cases—like the 1969 murder of Russell Goldstein, a Fall River antiques and arms dealer, who was shot late one night in his apartment above his retail store.

The murderers in these pages used guns, knives, axes, fists, fire, rope, and other tools—including their hands—to commit their dastardly deeds. Mothers killed their children, husbands and wives killed each other, and children murdered their parents. Police officers were killed in cold blood while doing their jobs. Deaths occurred in physicians' offices during abortions, and some victims were cut into pieces. Murders were committed in the suburbs and the city. Many of the accused were proclaimed insane—others committed suicide after the killing. Either the slayer went to jail, an insane asylum, or did themselves in by their own hand. Many did not serve a full prison term because they received pardons from the governor.

Murder does not discriminate. Victims and killers come from all races, nationalities, genders, and age groups. Many used drugs or sold drugs. Crimes of passion seemed to outweigh robberies but there were still many of those. Some killers were just "bad" people who did not regret their actions and had no qualms about how they slayed their victims.

There were cult murders and unsolved roadside killings of young women believed to be prostitutes. Some of our murderers were released to kill additional innocent victims. It seems that there was only one sex crime of a minor, death resulting, in the woods in Freetown. It took four trials before the perpetrator was convicted and sentenced, and he eventually died in prison. During that time, the family of the child was subjected to reliving the event again and again.

There were quiet decades and during other times it seemed like murder was rampant, as in the 1990s—but that is for another volume. Every year in that decade saw multiple killings—primarily a result of drugs and gangs, which were introduced into the SouthCoast during the 1980s.

I never realized how many slayings took place in the area over the years until I began my research. There were over fifty murders in the suburbs and 200 in the city of Fall River. Seventy-five women and children were killed and 172 men. The victims are now in a better place and some of the killers are back out on the streets after serving their sentence. Many have moved away from the area and some have passed on to their just reward. Some still remain behind bars and I have encountered local correctional officers who have related their present behavior.

It was my intention to honor victims and law enforcement by writing this book. I wanted to keep their memories alive and not simply recall them as statistics. The time is now to stop the hate. Stop the brutality. Stop the Murder, Manslaughter and Mayhem on the SouthCoast.

John B. "Red" Cummings, Jr.
June, 2017
Westport, MA

FOREWORD

John B. Cummings, Jr., has again demonstrated his abiding interest in the history, personages, and mores of his beloved Fall River and its SouthCoast environs. This work and the volume still to come involves the macabre subject of murder and mayhem, the tracing of over 245 cases from 1832 to the present time.

This overall work is divided into nine historical eras and each era is rendered in rich historical detail in a lucid style that illustrates the changing sociological background of the different periods of time. The author then capsulizes, in summary fashion, the ghastly and gruesome essence of each crime so that it can be easily grasped by the reader.

Some of the cases include the legendary Lizzie Borden double-ax murders that shocked Victorian Fall River and the world; the celebrated "Pinky" Hathaway case that scandalized the Depression Era southeast with its sexual overtones; the unsolved "roadside murders" of a series of young prostitutes in the 1980s; and the brutal drug and gang related assassinations of the gory 1990s.

The work is the result of exhaustive research, a two-year examination of the records of the Massachusetts Superior Court, the Fall River Historical Society, the Fall River Public Library, the *Fall River Herald News*, scholarly reference works on the history of the SouthCoast, and interviews with many authorities who are expert in law enforcement and in the history of Fall River and its changing social and economic patterns and customs.

The nineteenth century belief in moral progress was shattered by the catastrophic wars of the twentieth century. The horrendous killings endemic of twenty-first century urban life has established that our system of criminal law is inherently incapable of preventing murderous behavior or of successfully punishing it.

What is necessary for public peace is a return to traditional moral values, rooted in human nature and recognized by the light of conscience, which respect the sanctity and dignity of each human person. "Do unto others as you would have others do unto you" is the foundation of public order and the basis for the full and free exercise of personal rights. This work illustrates the disastrous social consequences when this precept is disdained and disregarded.

The underlying theme of this very instructive work is that virtuous behavior in conformity with deeply-held human values creates a society that is truly civil.

Edward F. Harrington
United States Senior District Judge

EDITOR'S NOTE

This book represents the first volume of a two-volume collection of murders on the SouthCoast. With over 250 cases detailed in both volumes, the grouping you have before you covers the years 1800 to 1969.

Each of the cases are arranged in a clearly delineated way, starting with the victim's name as the title, followed by vital information headings such as Crime, Victim, Accused, Details, The Trial, Outcome, Afterword, Addendum, Further Reading, and Gallery. The book attempts to lay out the information in a systematic way not only for ease of reading but also to enable ready reference lookups.

Some of these cases have been widely covered in the press. Consequently, these stories are more fleshed out than others because there is more information from many sources to help tell the story of the crime and the victim. Because this is a location-centric book (the SouthCoast), in many cases the only source of information is one or two local newspaper stories. In these instances, the material may seem thin, but the drama of the event is important nonetheless and deserves to be told.

The SouthCoast encompasses a wide swath of cities, towns, and communities in two states. These include, in Massachusetts: Acushnet, Berkley, Dartmouth, Fairhaven, Fall River, Freetown, Marion, Mattapoisett, New Bedford, Rochester, Somerset, Swansea, Wareham, and Westport. In Rhode Island, the communities included are Little Compton and Tiverton, because of their close proximity to the other towns and cities in Massachusetts.

This book does not purport to be a comprehensive compendium but, rather, a detailed sampling of the crimes that occurred. There will be omissions—mostly due to a lack of publicly available information. In each case, however, care has been taken to insure that the facts presented are as they have been previously reported. It is the wish of the author and editor that this book is an accurate representation of the murder, manslaughter, and mayhem on the SouthCoast.

Stefani Koorey, PhD

CHAPTER I
THE 1800S
THE BEGINNING

While not as unruly as the wild-wild West, the SouthCoast area of Massachusetts in the early 1800s was in the early stages of settlement, community building, and industry. Prior to the start of the Industrial Revolution, population numbers in the region fluctuated between 20,000 and 100,000 inhabitants. Industrial activity centered in the area later to be incorporated as the city of Fall River (in 1854). By 1850, Fall River had become a manufacturing center, with 11,000 residents and some 88,000 spindles—yet with this progress came a not-unexpected increased in social ills and violence.

In short order, Fall River became the cotton manufacturing center of the United States, and second only to Manchester, England, in the world, with a population in 1920 of 120,000. With improved rail and steam boat service, residents and visitors traveled freely between the city and Boston, Providence, Rhode Island, and New York City.

New Bedford, Massachusetts, the other city in the SouthCoast, was, during the 19th century, considered the most significant whaling port in the world. Incorporated as a city in 1847, New Bedford's diverse early population included those of English, Scottish, and Welsh origin, as well as Irish, Portugese-Azorian, and Cape Verdian. French-Canadians, Poles, and eastern Europeans arrived in the 20th century.

Population figures for New Bedford exceeded those of Fall River until the 1870s, when the Spindle City's industrial surge kicked in. It wasn't until the 1960s that New Bedford would beat their neighbors to the south, but only by a few thousand.

In the early days, the state lines between Rhode Island and Massachusetts were drawn differently and Tiverton, Rhode Island, and even Freetown, Massachusetts, claimed parts of Fall River, to the south and north, respectively.

Our first tragedy was, in fact, recorded in a section of Fall River that was, at the time of the incident, part of Tiverton, Rhode Island, on land owned by John Durfee, in an area later known as South Park and then, still later, Kennedy Park. This slaying, the first of many to be recorded in this book, never achieved the notoriety of the Borden murders later in the century, but the death of the pregnant young mill girl, who was hanged near a hay stack on the Durfee farm, and the minister who was twice tried and twice acquitted of the dastardly deed*, set the stage for hundreds of murders in the SouthCoast in the nineteenth, twentieth, and twenty-first centuries, and ushered in an unbroken history of violence that persists to this very day.

In this first chapter, which spans the full century, eighteen murders occurred on the SouthCoast. The century starts with Miss Sarah Cornell, just a few years prior to the great fire of 1843, and ends with the death of Police Officer Louis T. Gormley. Murder, manslaughter, and mayhem have indeed been a part of the fabric of the area for centuries. But other killings also deserve attention, not for the horrendous ways with which the perpetrators committed the acts but, rather, for the unfortunate victims whose vital lives were snuffed out by stabbings, shootings, drownings, abortions gone bad, and, in one very sad case, the throwing out of a baby from a window. Certainly, it is well known that axes were also a weapon of choice over the years.

Deadly brutality was not just restricted to the industrial centers of Fall River and New Bedford—the suburban towns of Freetown, Somerset, Dighton, Westport, and Swansea also participated. As the textile industry grew in Fall River, with fifteen new corporations and twenty-two new mills in production during the Civil War, immigrants from Ireland, the Azores, and Canada flocked to the city for work. By 1875, 14,000 people of the 125,000 inhabitants were working in the mills of Fall River on over one million spindles. The misuse of liquor, and later drugs, began to exert influence on the behavior of residents, with murder sometimes resulting.

As the cities of Fall River and New Bedford and the SouthCoast grew, building expansion ensued, with many now architecturally significant public and private homes constructed. Most mills in Fall River were built from granite quarried on site. Parks, schools, a public water supply, and sewage system complimented streetcar lines. The city was considered a transportation hub for the area because of its location—perfectly positioned for easy access to points north, south, east, and west. The world-famous Fall River Line became the connection between the rail line to Boston, Massachusetts, and steamship to New York City from 1847 to 1937. The SouthCoast became not only a location to travel through, but a place to travel to.

It feels as though in the last fifty years highlighted in the book (volume two), murders became more vicious, but that is just our modern understanding of crime. What could be more vicious than drowning your own child or throwing a baby out of a window to its death? While illegal drug use has certainly increased over the years and gangs exert their influence in the community, murder was more common in the 1800s than now. Ritual murders and the unidentified serial killer known as the New Bedford Highway Killer (1988-1989) stay close in our collective memories, but these more famous cases have joined the annals with common, everyday murders of passion, jealousy, and hate. Now it is time for you, the reader, to decide which time suffered the most. This outline of local murders only touches on motives. Much more detail needs to be explored. Let the sociologists and psychologists decide how and why these events took place. It is important to stress that, through this book, the victims have not been forgotten.

*Avery was acquitted once in court and once through a trial held by the Mothodist Church.

SARAH MARIA CORNELL

CRIME

The hanging death of a pregnant mill worker in the south end of Fall River, Massachusetts (then Tiverton, RI), on the John Durfee farm, on December 21, 1832.

VICTIM

Sarah Maria Cornell, 29

ACCUSED

Minister Ephraim Kingsbury Avery, married with an invalid wife and two children: Edwin, 5, and Catherine, an infant.

DETAILS

The victim was found hanging from a stack pole in an area of Tiverton, Rhode Island, which later became South Park in Fall River. The mill girl was four months pregnant and had been counseled by Rev. Ephraim K. Avery, a Methodist minister from Bristol, Rhode Island, who had met her in Lowell, Massachusetts, and later at a Methodist Camp in Connecticut. Among Cornell's effects was found a note she had written and dated the day of her death: "If I should be missing, enquire of Rev. Mr. Avery of Bristol, he will know where I am."

Suspicion centered on Reverend Avery when it was discovered that Cornell had conversations with a doctor indicating that the married Avery was the father of her unborn child. A coroner's jury determined that she had "committed suicide by hanging herself upon a stake ... and was influenced to commit said crime by the wicked conduct of a married man."

A second coroner's jury convened after the discovery of the pregnancy that accused Ephraim Kingsbury Avery, a married Methodist minister, as the probable "accessory" in her death. Avery was arrested but released on his own recognizance while he awaited trial.

At the inquest, two Justices of the Peace found that there was insufficient evidence to try Avery for the crime of murder. In response to public outrage, Harvey Harnden, the deputy sheriff of Fall River, Massachusetts, obtained an arrest warrant for Avery from a Rhode Island

Superior Court judge. When the warrant was served, it was discovered that Avery had fled.

Harnden tracked Avery to New Hampshire and took him back to Newport, Rhode Island, to await his trial in jail. On May 8, 1833, Avery was indicted for murder by a Newport County grand jury, to which he pleaded "not guilty."

THE TRIAL

There were two trials where Reverend Avery was accused of murder. The first was convened on May 6, 1833. It lasted twenty-seven days. Due to Rhode Island law at the time, Avery was not allowed to give testimony in his own defense. On June 2, 1833, the jury found Ephraim Kingsbury Avery "not guilty." After his acquittal, Avery returned to his position as a minister in the Methodist Church. However, public scorn was high and rallies were organized that hanged and burned effigies of Avery. The Reverend himself was almost lynched in Boston. The Methodist Church's New England Conference convened a trial, and once again Avery was acquitted.

OUTCOME

The murder remains unsolved.

AFTERWORD

In 1836, Avery left the ministry and moved first to Connecticut, then upstate New York, finally settling with his family to Ohio, where he became a farmer. He died in 1869 in Ohio, where he is buried in South Pittsfield Cemetery, Lorain County, Ohio. Sarah Cornell was buried on the farm near where her body was discovered. Many years later when the farm was annexed to Massachusetts and became part of Fall River and the farm became South Park, her body was exhumed and moved to Oak Grove Cemetery where it remains in Plot 2733 on Whitethorn Path to this date.

FURTHER READING

Kasserman, David Richard. *Fall River Outrage: Life, Murder, and Justice in Early Industrial New England*. Philadelphia: University of Pennsylvania Press, 1986.

"Nothing in Annals of Fall River Attracted As Much Attention as Borden Murder Case," *Fall River Herald News* (Fall River, Massachusetts), September 19, 1958.

Raven, Rory. *Wicked Conduct: The Minister, The Mill Girl, and the Murder that Captivated Old Rhode Island*. SC: History Press, 2009.

Williams, Catherine Read. *Fall River: An Authentic Narrative*. Boston: Lilly, Wait & Col, 1834.

Verses written in Honour of Sarah Maria Cornell:

And here thou masks thy lonely bed,
Thou poor forlorn and injured one;
Here rests thy aching head—
Marked by a nameless stone.

Poor victim of man's lawless passion,
Though e'er so tenderly caress—
Better to trust the raging ocean,
Than lean upon his stony breast.

And thou though frail, wert fair and mild;
Some gentle virtues warmed thy breast.
Poor outcast being! sorrow's child!
Reproach can't break thy rest.
On thy poor wearied breast the turf
Lies quite as soft as on the rich:
What now to thee the scorn and mirth,
Of sanctimonious hypocrites.

That mangled form now finds repose,
And who shall say thy soul does not,
Since he who from the grave arose
Brought immortality to light.

Poor fated one the day is coming
When sin and sorrow pass away—
I see the light already gleaming
Which ushers in an endless day.

Where shall the murderer be found?
He calls upon the rocks in vain—
The force of guilt will then confound,
Alas the 'Judge! no longer man.

He calls upon the rocks in vain—
The adamantine rocks recoil,
Earth can no longer hide the slain,
And death yields up his spoil.

Where shall thy murderer appear?
My God thy judgments are most deep:
No verdict can the monster clear
Who dies a hypocrite must wake to weep.

Appeared first in the *Fall River Monitor*, reprinted in Catherine
Williams' *Fall River, An Authenic Narrative* (1834).

The Ballad of Avery's Knot:

"This ballad was written in 1833 by an old English woman who was living near the Coal Mines, in Portsmouth, Rhode Island, just down the Narragansett Bay from Fall River."

Young virgins all a warning take,
  Remember Avery's knot.
Enough to make your heart to ache,
  Don't let it be forgot.
You mothers that have infants
  To sympathize and mourn.
Such murder never was done here
  Or ever yet was known.
He killed the mother and the child.
  What a wicked was he!
The Devil helped him all the while.
  How wicked he must be.
He dragged her round upon the ground
  Till she no noise could make.
Contrived a lot—tied Avery's knot—
  And hung her to a stake.
The Devil he was standing by,
  A laughing in his sleeve.
It is so plain he can't deny,
  He must not be reprieved.
He preached the Gospel night and day.
  What a wicked man was he.
The Devil helped him preach and pray,
  How wicked he must be.
How could he stand and preach and pray
  With murder in his heart;
The Devil helped him day by day
  And he will make him smart.
Methodism he did profess
  For that was his belief.
How can he ever take a rest.
  He must not be reprieved.
Hang him, hang him, on a tree.
  Tie round him Avery's knot.
Forever let him hanged be
  And never be forgot.

From Alice Brayton, *Life on the Stream*, Volume One, 1962.

GALLERY

Illustration of poem titled "Lines in Commemoration of the Death of Sarah M. Cornell by Mr. John Thomas. Broadside, W. Johnson, Printer.

"View of Durfee's Farm, with the stack yard, &c. at Fall-River."

REPORT

OF THE

TRIAL

OF THE

REV. EPHRAIM K. AVERY,

METHODIST MINISTER,

FOR THE

MURDER

OF

SARAH MARIA CORNELL,

AT TIVERTON,

IN THE

COUNTY OF NEWPORT, RHODE ISLAND,

BEFORE THE SUPREME JUDICIAL COURT OF THAT STATE,

MAY 6th, 1833.

Containing the evidence of the numerous witnesses unabridged, and the speeches of General Albert C. Greene, Attorney General; the Hon. D. Pearce, and William R. Staples, Esq., Counsel for the Prosecution; and those of the Hon. J. Mason, Richard R. Randolph, Esq., and other Counsel for the Prisoner; together with the charge of

HIS HONOR CHIEF JUSTICE EDDY,

IN FULL, AS TAKEN IN SHORT HAND, BY

A LAW REPORTER OF NEW-YORK.

———— " Murder,
" Though it hath no tongue, will speak
" As with a most miraculous organ."

New=York,

PUBLISHED BY WILLIAM STODART, 6 CORTLANDT-ST.

"A very bad man." 1833 print.

REV. EPHRAIM K. AVERY.

From "The Correct, Full and Impartial Report of the Trial of Rev. Ephraim K. Avery, before the Supreme Judicial Court of the State of Rhode-Island, at Newport, May 6, 1933, for the Murder of Sarah Cornell"

ASA CLARK, JR.

CRIME

Murder in Freetown, Massachusetts, by sharp implement, of the son of a constable of Freetown, Massachusetts, on October 23, 1838.

VICTIM

Asa Clark, Jr., 22 (born March 18, 1816)

ACCUSED

Benjamin Cummings, 28

DETAILS

According to the *Law Reporter* (1840), "a warrant had been obtained against [Benjamin Cummings] as a common drunkard, on the complaint of the deceased, and had been given to a deputy of the sheriff, who made an attempt to arrest him, but [Cummings] keeping out of the way, the deputy failed in his object, and delivered the warrant to Asa Clark, Sr., the father of the deceased, who was a constable of Freetown, and had been for many years. When Cummings learned that Clark had the warrant, he declared that he would not be taken alive; that neither old Clark or his son should take him; that if an attempt was made, he would use his knife, club or axe; and these threats were made at various times, to many witnesses, in different language, but all strongly expressive of the prisoner's intention to take the life of the officer or his assistants, if any attempt was made to execute the precept.

"It was proved on one occasion, while Clark had the warrant, [Cummings] came to the road side, before his house, so placing himself with his knife in his hand, that Clark was afraid to arrest him, and there had been a conversations with him about the warrant; and Clarke [sic] told him that if he kept quiet and behaved tolerably well he would not serve the warrant; that he expected he would get drunk, but if he was not too quarrelsome and malicious no notice would be taken of it, and then complained that his two horses had been killed by somebody, who cut their throats in the night time, and that such conduct was too bad, and could not be allowed. [Cummings] promised to behave well, and it was then understood if he did he should not be troubled with the warrant; and Clark thereupon took it from his hat, where he usually carried it, and put it elsewhere in his house.

"On the night of October 23d, after Clarke [sic] had retired to bed, he was awakened by one of his neighbors, and told that [Cummings] and his brothers were out, and in all probability intended to do mischief. Clark, thereupon, with his son, and the neighbor who thus called him up, and two others who came out on like information, went to the barn, in fear that it might be set on fire, and there searched for some time. They presently saw [Cummings] and his brother Joel pass down, —heard them converse together, —and after some time saw them return, and both throw large stones at Clark's house. Clark having at some intermediate time placed his warrant in his hat again, had it with him, and resolved to arrest [Cummings], and called on his son Asa and the others to assist him. They accordingly proceeded to do so. Joel having passed on, young Clark, after some remarks, went up to [Cummings], who had a stick in his hand, which he threw away, and turned round, facing young Clark, who seized him round the body, and both fell. Immediately after, young Clark cried out that he was stabbed; he got up and was assisted into the house, and soon after died of the wound, which was inflicted by a sharp instrument penetrating into his body, through which the intestines were protruded."

THE TRIAL

Law Reporter stated that "evidence, corroborated in essential particulars by the dying declaration of the deceased, was directly contradicted by Joel Cummings and his sister, but their testimony was impeached by the government. It was contended by [Cummings'] counsel, on their testimony, that [Cummings] had an axe at the time, and that the wound was inflicted by an accidental fall upon it. The physician, however, after examining the pantaloons worn by the deceased, that the cut made in them, declared that the wound could not have been made by an axe.

"It was objected that the warrant of arrest being

interlined and erased, and especially that the direction to the constable, being to a constable of New Bedford, which word was printed and erased, and Freetown inserted, could not be deemed a legal warrant unless it was shown that the alterations were made before service.

"On this point it was in evidence by the testimony of Clark, that the warrant had never been altered since it came into his possession, and it was admitted to be duly signed by the magistrate.

"The court said it was to be taken to be a genuine warrant until the contrary was shown by [Cummings]. It was further objected that unless the constable had the warrant about his person, he had no right to arrest the party.

"The court decided that it was not necessary for the officer to have his precept about his person when he made an arrest, provided it was in some convenient place to be shown to the party who might desire to see it.

"The mode of arrest was objected to as unnecessarily violent. This was left to the jury, with instructions that an officer might use all necessary force, as well as to prevent an attack which he had reason to anticipate, as to render it harmless.

"The jury found [Cummings] guilty, and on a subsequent day he was sentenced to suffer death.

"In pronouncing his sentence, the Chief Justice made a very pathetic and kind address to [Cummings], calculated to awaken him to a sense of his crime, and the awful situation to which it had brought him."

OUTCOME

Cummings was hanged on August 7, 1839, after being convicted of the murder.

According to a friend, as reported in the Vermont *Union Whig* (1844), Cummings "had never enjoyed the advantages of even a common school education, and at the time of the trial, I believe, he could not read. He was intemperate, and moved in the lowest grade of society.

"He declared his ignorance of the deed. He was tried at Taunton and condemned, mainly upon the testimony of a single witness, and that witness was the father of the deceased. After the trial I frequently visited him. He always declared that he knew not how the deed was done. I learned, on enquiry, that Clark, the principal witness in the case, was an enemy of the prisoner, and had been so more than 20 years.

"On examining his testimony I was convinced that he had sworn that he saw which he could not have beheld, on that unusually dark night. I, moreover, learned, that he was anxious to have the prisoner hung. I was now led to believe that the wound which Clark died was purely accidental. Perhaps while some persons who were on the ground, in the scuffle, intended to wound Cummings, Clark was, by mistake killed.

"Petitions were sent to the Executive, praying that he might not be executed.—With several other persons I went before the Governor and Council, to plead for the prisoner. To my utter astonishment, Asa Clark, the father of the deceased, appeared there with Elnathan P. Hathaway, a lawyer of Freetown, and urged the Executive to hang Cummings. The efforts of the petitioners were unavailing.

"A gallows was erected in the Taunton jail, near the door of the prisoner's cell.—Fourteen persons were present to witness the bloody scene. Every thing being prepared, the sheriff threw his arms around the neck of the prisoner, and said to him— "Cummings, you now are about to die; are you innocent or guilty?" "I know not," said he, "how the deed was done." A few days after the execution, the sheriff informed that he verily believed that the man was innocent of the crime for which he had executed him. I think had Cummings done the deed he would have manufactured some story to deceive the people, or when he saw there was no chance to escape the gallows, he would have confessed that he was guilty. Probably he was an innocent person.

J.M.S."

AFTERWORD

Asa Clark, Sr., died on February 29, 1864 at the age of 84, after spending his later years as a farmer.

FURTHER READING

Chandler, P.W., Editor. *Law Reporter*, Volume II. Chandler. Boston: Weeks, Jordan and Company, 1840. Pp. 83-85.
J.M.S. *Union Whig* (Rutland, Vermont), December 19, 1844.
"Nothing in Annals of Fall River Attracted As Much Attention as Borden Murder Case," *Fall River Herald News* (Fall River, Massachusetts), September 19, 1958.

GALLERY

Town and City Clerks of Massachusetts. Massachusetts Vital and Town Records. Provo, UT: Holbrook Research Institute (Jay and Delene Holbrook). (Ancestry.com)

Town and City Clerks of Massachusetts. Massachusetts Vital and Town Records. Provo, UT: Holbrook Research Institute (Jay and Delene Holbrook). (Ancestry.com)

HOLDER AND ELIZA BORDEN

CRIME

Two young children drowned in a cistern in their home basement at 68 Second Street, Fall River, Massachusetts, by their mother, who then took her own life, on May 4, 1848.

VICTIMS

Holder Borden and Eliza Borden, 6 months and 3 years old

ACCUSED

Eliza Darling Borden, 37, mother (Mrs. Lodowick Borden)

DETAILS

According to the *Fall River Weekly News*, a "most melancholy occurrence" transpired at 68 Second Street, on May 4, 1848, between the hours of 4 and 5. Eliza Borden, the second wife to Lodowick Borden, uncle to Andrew J. Borden, "took her two youngest children, went down cellar, and drowned them in the cistern; then stepping behind the chimney, cut her own throat with a razor, and died almost instantly." The only offspring that was spared was the couple's eldest daughter, Maria.

According to the *Public Ledger*, "Mrs. Borden has within a few days shown undeniable evidence of an unsound mind, expressing fears that they should come to want, though her husband was in good circumstances. Yesterday afternoon, a girl who lived with Mrs. Borden, went out to get a pail of water. On her return, Mrs. Borden and the two younger children were missing. She asked an older child where her mother had gone, and was told that she had gone into the cellar. She went to the cellar door, but was afraid to enter upon hearing the groans of Mrs. B. The neighbors were called in, and found Mrs. B. extended on the floor, with her throat cut and just alive. The children were both dead in the cistern. This dreadful tragedy has caused a great excitement in Fall River, and a deep sympathy is felt for Mr. Borden in this sudden and dreadful bereavement."

ADDENDUM

In our modern understanding of mental health issues, it is entirely possible that Eliza Darling Borden suffered from post partum depression. Her last child was born six months before the act which resulted in three deaths. In 2001, Andrea Yates was found guilty of killing her five children by drowning them in a bathtub. Although she was previously diagnosed with postpartum psychosis, it was ruled that she was capable of discerning right from wrong and sentenced to serving life in prison. Regardless, according to *Psychology Today*, "Infanticide is a very rare phenomenon; only about 4 percent of women who become psychotic kill their babies."

It was reported by those who knew her that Eliza "committed the lamentable deed in a paroxysm of insanity" and had been "considered a little out her head for a few days past."

These murders occurred in the house next door to 92 Second Street, where, in 1892, Andrew J. and Abby Borden were hatcheted to death. At the time of the killing of these children, Andrew Borden was 26 years old and resided in his father's home at 12 Ferry Street. It was not until 1872 that the Andrew J. Borden family would move to Second Street.

A cistern is an underground reservoir for collecting rainwater. According to OldHouseWeb.com, cisterns in 19th century homes, used "the roof as a rain collection surface," with gutters and downspouts delivering the water to the cistern." Although some were manufactured of iron, steel or made of wood, most were constructed below ground of brick or stone. They could be made watertight with an interior parge coat of hydraulic cement. After about 1900, formed concrete was sometimes used. The masonry cistern chamber could be shaped like a vault, bell, beehive, jug or flat-topped with a wooden platform for the cover ... most were built against the home's foundation and water was drawn from a tap located low on the basement wall. Some delivered the water with a hand pump. The water, not of the quality for drinking, was mainly used for washing and laundry ... Although rare, there's some remaining evidence of filtering the collected water. Some cisterns are divided into two or more chambers encouraging debris to settle and finer particles were filtered out as the water passed through porous brick or stone partitions. Some partitions were made with an interior cavity and animal charcoal, also called "bone black," filled the space, further purifying the collected water."

FURTHER READING

"A Distressing Occurrence." *Poughkeepsie Journal* (Poughkeepsie, New York), May 13, 1848.

"Cisterns—Historic Water Conservation." oldhouseweb.com/blog/cisterns-historic-water-conservation

"Dreadful Tragedy." *Public Ledger* (Philadelphia, Pennsylvania), May 6, 1848.

Fall River Weekly News, May 4, 1848.

Martins, Michael and Dennis Binette. *Parallel Lives: A Social History of Lizzie A. Borden and Her Fall River*. Fall River Historical Society, 2010.

"Melancholy Affair." *The Vermont Union Whig* (Rutland, Vermont), May 11, 1848.

"Moms Who Kill." *Psychology Today*, November 1, 2002. psychologytoday.com/articles/200211/moms-who-kill

"A Tragical Affair." *Buffalo Weekly Republic* (Buffalo, New York), May 9, 1848.

"Tragical Event." *Washington Telegraph* (Washington, Arkansas), June 7, 1848.

GALLERY

Second Street looking north from corner of Spring Street, 1893. The house where the Borden children were murdered in the cistern in on the far right. The next building to the left is the Andrew J. Borden house. *Phillips History of Fall River.*

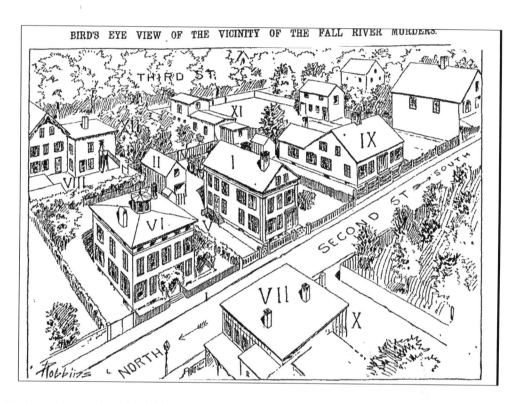

The Borden house where the children were murdered in the cistern in 1848 appears here as designated with an IX. The Andrew J. Borden house, where Andrew and Abby Borden were murdered in 1893, is marked with an I. *Boston Daily Globe*, August 11, 1982.

GIDEON MANCHESTER

CRIME	Police Constable shot and killed in Fall River, Massachusetts, on July 16, 1852.
VICTIM	Police Constable Gideon Manchester, 35
ACCUSED	James Clough, 29

DETAILS   Gideon Manchester confronted James Clough who was observed breaking and entering into local Fall River businesses and stealing approximately $500 in cash in the early morning hours at the end of Manchester's watch. When Constable Manchester attempted to place him under arrest, Clough ran and "gave Manchester, a 200-pounder, a merry chase which ended on Greene Street" (*Fall River Herald News*). Clough then drew a pistol and fired, mortally wounding Constable Manchester.

THE TRIAL   The suspect was arrested and convicted of murdering badge #52 and sent to prison on December 30, 1852.

OUTCOME   James Clough was executed in Taunton, Massachusetts, by hanging on April 28, 1854, after multiple escape attempts from jail. He was considered a problem inmate by law enforcement and was chained and handcuffed in a dungeon in Charlestown, Massachusetts prison. According the *Brooklyn Daily Eagle*, at his hanging, "fifty persons were admitted as spectators. The Rev. Messrs. Emery, Blodgett and Maltby were with the prisoner in his cell most of the morning. Clough, who was 29 years of age, and unmarried, met his fate without exhibiting any perceptible emotion."

AFTERWORD   Gideon Manchester was survived by his mother, wife, and three young children. Manchester was a butcher during the daytime.

This was the first of four police killings during the history of the Fall River Police Department included in this book.

FURTHER READING

"Constable Gideon Manchester." Officer Down Memorial Page. odmp.org.

"Execution of James Clough." *Brooklyn Daily Eagle* (Brooklyn, New York), April 29, 1854.

"Nothing in Annals of Fall River Attracted As Much Attention as Borden Murder Case," *Fall River Herald News* (Fall River, Massachusetts), September 19, 1958.

Racine, Daniel (former Fall River Chief of Police). Personal Interview. 2016.

ISAIAH "JOHN" BULLOCK

CRIME	Robbery and murder in Freetown, Massachusetts, on June 20, 1862.
VICTIM	Isaiah "John" Bullock, 46
ACCUSED	Obed Reynolds, 18
DETAILS	

According to *The Evening Standard* (June 20, 1862), "About seven o'clock last evening the body of John Bullock ... was found ... shockingly mangled. It was evident from the appearance of the ground in the vicinity that a desperate struggle had taken place. Blood was found in his wagon and in considerable quantity on both sides of the road. There were several buckshot wounds on the lower part of the face, and a serious stab in the abdomen, and one on the neck and a dozen or more in the breast, probably penetrating no farther than the bone. There was also a cut on the upper part of the head, extending back 5 or 6 inches from the forehead, laying open the flesh to the bone. His watch valued at $100 was missing, also his pocketbook, but a sum of money amounting to $10 was found in his pocket. It is not known how much money he had with him at the time.

"The body was found by two peddlers who alarmed the neighbors. It was taken to an unoccupied house called the Crapo house, set about one and one half miles from where the murder was committed.

"Coroner William O. Russell of this city was sent for, and arrived at the scene about 3 o'clock this morning and took charge of the body. After a cursory examination, the selectmen of Freetown and Dr. Nicholas being present, the coroner permitted the removal of the body to the late residence where it arrived at an early hour this morning.

"Mr. Bullock left his home early yesterday morning and was last seen near Assonet about 5 ½ o'clock in the afternoon where he had some conversation with a woman with reference to a piece of land he wished to purchase. While he was talking with her a man was seen to pass, having a gun with him, and suspicions are entertained that he might be the murderer. Mr. Bullock soon after left, it is supposed, for home and was waylaid in the woods on the way.

"It was thought he might have been shot and then either fell or jumped from the wagon, when the horrid work was finished with a knife. As he was a very powerfully-built man some think more than one person engaged in the murder. But, of course, nothing is known as to this, and with the advantage of arms and the surprise and shot wounds, one man might easily have accomplished the deed.

"A piece of stick, supposed to be a part of the ramrod of the gun, was found near the place of the tragedy, which may lead to the detection of the murderer. The City Marshal and Deputy Sheriff Hurlbut are upon the alert and we hope they may be successful in their pursuit. Mr. Bullock was about 46 years of age.

"The Coroner's inquest was assembled in his residence in Bellville today at 10 a.m. ... Dr. C.D. Stickney proceeded to make a post mortem examination. About 20 shots took effect on the face and neck to, some passing completely through from one side of the neck to the other. Twenty five stab wounds in all were found on the body, several of them being mortal. Three or four of the stabs on the breast, which on slight inspection appeared to be superficial, penetrated the lungs.

"About one o'clock the jury adjourned to 2 ½ o'clock when they will proceed to Freetown to view the scene of the murder."

According to Arthur Sherman Phillips in his *History of Fall River*, "About five hundred feet from the extreme northeasterly city line in the Copicut section, yet two miles from Copicut village, near the Bullock Road, which leads from Assonet to New Bedford, in a rough barren section stands a rough granite post. ... It marks the spot where in June, 1862, one Isaiah Bullock was murdered by a seventeen year old lad named Obed Reynolds. This murder caused widespread consternation because the dissolute youth, seeking only to possess a few dollars was lying in wait for a drygoods and grocery peddler whose weekly route caused him to pass through the lonely road, which in fact he had traversed the previous day. When Bullock happened along returning to his New Bedford home, in a democrat wagon, from the delivery of a barrel of rum to a kitchen barroom at Slab Bridge [Freetown, Massachusetts], knowing Bullock and his business, the youth held him up, blinded him with a gun shot and then during a scuffle which followed, during which the gun was wrested from him, he stabbed Bullock to death. The facts were related to me by my friend Paul Burns of Assonet ... Mr. Burns was helping his father on the latter's farm, which was a mile easterly on the Chace Road. Burns heard the noise of the scuffle, then supposing it was from an intervening farm where a neighbor was berating his oxen. Reynolds returned to his home and his father turned him over to the police."

According to Walter E. Clark, in an interview conducted in 1934, his father, Thomas H. Clark, figured in the story. Clark's father spoke to Obed Reynolds as the lad was walking along the road that fateful day, gun under arm.

Walter Clark, at the time of the murder "a mere boy playing about the farm on the warm June afternoon," related that his father told him that after Obed had reached home, he hid for a time "under his bed and did other peculiar things to arouse suspicion of his father, Noah Reynolds ... [Obed], intending to get married, was sorely in need of money. He was young, and like many other boys of his years, had little or nothing in his own right."

"It was believed by Clark that Reynolds' long yearning for cash, coupled with his drinking, caused him to commit the brutal crime. Clark added that the youth was quoted as saying after his arrest that he 'mixed gunpowder with rum to give him courage.'"

THE TRIAL

Writes Phillips, [Reynolds] "was indicted for murder June 19, 1982, at Freetown." According to the *New Bedford Standard Times*, "An indictment charging murder in three counts was returned against the Freetown youth at the December term of the Superior Court here in 1862. The first count which set forth in a profusion of words that death was caused by shotgun wounds was nol prossed [will not proceed]. The second and third counts pertained to death by the stab wounds. He was convicted on the second count. The court sustained the contention that the cause of death was due to the stabbing, and therefore proceeded on that finding. ... The youth pleaded not guilty April 24, 1863 ... Trial began May 19 at Taunton ... It lasted until May 21 when the 12 good men and true brought in a verdict of murder in the first degree."

OUTCOME

There was a verdict of guilty in the Supreme Judicial Court, after which Reynolds was sentenced to be hanged by the neck until he was dead.

AFTERWORD

On January 7, 1864, Reynolds' death sentence was commuted to life imprisonment by Governor John A. Andrew.

According to the *New Bedford Standard Times*, "Mr. Clark recalled that young Reynolds developed tuberculosis during his incarceration and died about six months after the commutation of his sentence to life imprisonment."

Clark reported that Zeph Clark "put up the stone to designate the murder spot. Legendary only is the story that originally the date of the murder was carved in the stone, and chiseled out soon after by persons friendly with the family of the slayer."

FURTHER READING

Mahoney, Francis C. "Murder of New Bedford Wine Merchant Recalled." *New Bedford Standard Times*, June, 1934.

"Murder and Highway Robbery in Freetown." *The Evening Standard*, June 20, 1862.

Phillips, Arthur Sherman. *Phillips History of Fall River. Fascicle III.* Fall River, Dover Press, 1946.

"Vice and Ignorance in Massachusetts." *Pittsburgh Daily Post* (Pittsburgh, Pennsylvania), February 27, 1864.

GALLERY

Bullock rock from 1962. *Photo courtesy of Barry French.*

Bullock rock from 1962. *Photo courtesy of Barry French.*

Bullock rock as it stands today, more of a yard ornament than historical marker.
Photo courtesy of Stefani Koorey.

BENJAMIN HOWARD

CRIME	Robbery and murder on a farm in Westport, Massachusetts, on November 29, 1870.
VICTIM	Benjamin Howard, 82
ACCUSED	Charles Cuffee, 15
DETAILS	

According to th *Burlington Free Press*, "On Thursday afternoon it was remarked by several farmers near by that 'Uncle Ben' had not been seen for a few days, and on Friday there were some inquiries concerning his whereabouts. On Saturday the neighbors, becoming somewhat alarmed, though[t] best to make a search for him.

"At the south end of the house, beneath the underpinning, a milk pail, filled with milk, was found, and beside it, the old man's cap. On the search being continued, the searching party discovered blood stains leading to a meadow south-west of the house, over a stone wall into a field, and over still another wall, partially thrown down, into the woods a few feet distant. Following this trail into the woods about thirty feet, the searchers found the dead body of the old man, with is right leg severed from his body at the thigh, and missing. A search for the missing limb was then made, and it was finally discovered in the woods, partially covered with leaves, a few feet south of the body. It was also discovered that an attempt had been made to break open the back door with an iron bar, three marks of its insertion being plainly visible between the door and the casing.

"Upon taking the body into the house and removing the garments, it was ascertained that Mr. Howard had been shot through the arm. He had also been struck four times in the head with an axe. Two of these wounds were between the eyes and about two inches long. These were evidently done with the edge of the axe. One of the other two was near the left temple and fractured the skull.

"The truth concerning this horrible murder has probably been elicited in a confession by a colored boy of 15 called Cuff [sic], whose true name is said to be Hall. He says he took his gun about four o'clock in the morning, and proceeded to the house of the old man Howard, which he tried to enter by means of a crowbar, but, fearing to alarm Mr. Howard, hid behind a wall and waited until he returned from milking, when he shot him. The old man said, 'What are you about?' and walked as far as the front door, when he fell backwards on the doorstep. The boy then struck him twice on the head with a wooden wash-pounder, which he found near the house, and killed him. Hall took the wallet, in which he found $12.50 and the key, and performed the mutilation of the old man's remains and hid them where found, then returned home, the whole deed occupying about three hours. He does not appear to realize the magnitude of his crime, but says he was ashamed and sorry that he killed Howard, when he saw the body on Saturday."

A lengthy story about the crime that appeared in *The New York Herald* states that the "colored boy, aged about fifteen years, named Charles Horatio Cuff [sic], who lives a short distance from Howard's house and near where the cart track leaves the cross road had been seen with money in his possession, and that he was suspected of having stolen the old man's watch some time ago. They boy was known to have changed a ten dollar bill at a store at the Head of Westport on Friday last, and he expended it in a foolish manner, buying prize peanut packages to a great extent and then giving the gifts which they contained to his acquaintances."

"The possession of so much money naturally attracted the attention of the people in the vicinity, and considerable talk was made in regard to it. In the course of conversation the officers also ascertained that Cuff [sic] left his house early on Tuesday morning, say about four o'clock. These circumstances excited their suspicions, and going to a school, which Cuff [sic] attended, and where he was yesterday morning, they pretended to have lost the road, saying they were anxious to visit the scene of the murder. Cluff's [sic] services as a guide were secured, and Mr. Marston with Captain Perry and officer Dayton, drove to Howard's house. The boy, well acquainted with the premises, showed the three strangers about the place, telling the facts of the discovery of the murder, as previously published, and appearing but little concerned at several sharp and telling suggestions made by the officers.

Here the reporting adds a new character to the account. "His story is substantially as follows:—He has been intimate with a boy named John Pettis, about his own age, and who lives near by, and the two boys knew that Howard had quite a sum of money on his person. Cuff [sic] robbed the old man of his watch, as the people suspected, and the two boys were thoroughly acquainted with the habits of the old man and the premises. The boys apparently had considerable talk in regard to the money and on Monday of last week they met, when Pettis suggested that Cuff should take a pistol which Pettis owned, break into Howard's house at night, cover himself with a bedquilt so the old man would not know him, and obtain the money, shooting Howard in case he was discovered. This Cuff [sic] declined to do, saying that Pettis wanted to have him do all the work, and that his own people would find him out, and finally the boys separated with the understanding that Pettis should undertake the robbery on Tuesday morning, and that Cuff [sic] should be there to assist him.

"On Tuesday morning, Cuff [sic] says about four o'clock, he woke up just as a pistol shot was fired. Telling his mother he was going to see about some traps, he hurried to Howard's house just as Pettis struck the old man with an ax on the doorsteps of the house. He then saw Pettis drag the body to the barn and endeavor to get it through. At that time Cuff [sic] was discovered by the other boy, who called to him for assistance. This assistance Cuff [sic] willingly rendered, and the body was dragged into the meadow, where it was searched. The old man's wallet, a key, a knife, and some tobacco were found in the pocket of his pants. Pettis took possession of the money and key, and the other articles were left on the body. The boys then commenced the grave, digging alternately, until Cuff [sic] says, it began to grow light and they were alarmed.

"The corpse was placed in the grave, but it was not deep enough, and Cuff [sic] took it out. The boys then had a consultation, and finally Pettis went to the house and obtained the saw and ax, and while Cuff [sic] watched Pettis cut off the leg. Cuff [sic] says they could not drag him on the wall, for he was very heavy, and that was the reason for severing the limb. The boys then hurriedly carried the remains into the woods, partially covered them with leaves and left them.

"On the way home Pettis told Cuff [sic] that he was hid behind a wall when Howard came from the barn with the milk pail. The old man saw him and asked him what he was doing there. Pettis made no reply, but fired at him just as he reached the door step. The old man sat down his milk pail and then fell. Pettis ran and attacked the victim with an axe, and at that moment Cuff [sic] appeared on the scene.

"Cuff [sic] says Pettis gave him a ten dollar bill and some script on the way home, but does not know how much money he retained. The wallet, pistol and key were thrown in the woods. On Sunday night Pettis cautioned Cuff [sic] against telling anything. Cuff [sic] said Pettis was very much frightened and quivering all over while they were handling Howard, but that he did not feel scared.

"Cuff [sic] is a boy about five feet eight inches in height and is not very strongly built. He has a thorough negro face, with a very low forehead and thick bushy hair. His answers to the numerous questions of the officers displayed considerable cunning, and he does not appear to be impressed with the magnitude of the deed. His story was carefully prepared, but not plausible enough, and the close questioning of the officers soon broke it down, and the above narrative, drawn out by piecemeal, was obtained.

"Having thus obtained a clue to the other party in the terrible tragedy, the officers, at half-past one this morning, started for Westport to arrest Pettis, and the announcement has just been received that they were successful, and they will undoubtedly arrive here with the young murderer in the cours[e] of the evening, and the preliminary examination will probably be held to-morrow."

Still another version of the story is told by Cukie Macomber that states that the murderer of Benjamin Howard was actually William Davol, 20, who had just been released from prison for robbery. The police did not pursue the story because Charles had already confessed.

According to Macomber, "that while tending his trap line [Charles Cufee] met William Davol near the Howard farm. Will asked if he could borrow Charles' BB gun for a few minutes. A shot was fired and Charles went in the direction of the sound and found Will hitting Ben with a laundry pounder and an axe. Will offered Charles twelve dollars if he would help him drag the body into the woods but a swearing of secrecy was required first. Twleve dollars was a lot of money so Charles agreed. A leg had to be hacked off when it became entangled in a fence. Charles said he confessed to the crime earlier because he had promised not to mention Will. He had accused John Petty because John knew about what happened and he hoped John would implicate Will. That way Charles could keep his promise to Will. William Davol and John Petty testified that they knew nothing of the crime."

THE TRIAL

Charles Cuffee was charged with murder in the first degree before a jury in Taunton, Massachusetts. He later retracted his confession but was prosecuted for the crime regardless. He was found guilty of murder in the first degree.

OUTCOME

The judge ordered that the "young black boy be hung by the neck until dead."

AFTERWORD

Charles Cuffee's sentence was commuted by Governor Claflin of Massachusetts to life in prison because of his youth and lack of education, but, on August 28, 1874, he died of pneumonia.

FURTHER READING

"Horrible Murder in Massachusetts." *The Baltimore Sun* (Baltimore, Maryland), December 6, 1870.

Macomber, Cukie. (No Subject). E-mail.

"Murderer Arrested." *Titusville Herald* (Titusville, Pennsylvania), December 7, 1870.

"Remarkable Murder in Massachusetts." *Evening Star* (Washington, District of Columbia), December 9, 1870.

"The Westport (Mass.) Butchery." *The New York Herald* (New York, New York), December 7, 1870.

"Tragedy in Massachusetts." *Burlington Free Press* (Burlington, Vermont), December 12, 1870.

GEORGE H. THYNG

CRIME

Wife accused of poisoning her husband in New Bedford, Massachusetts, on July 9, 1875.

VICTIM

George H. Thyng, 32

ACCUSED

Rosalie A. Thyng, 23

DETAILS

George H. Thyng had been sick for two weeks when he died. He lived in New Bedford with his second wife, Rosalie A. (Wordell) Thyng. At the autopsy, large quantities of arsenic were found in Mr. Thyng's stomach and other parts of his body. According to the *Boston Post* (May 25, 1876), "Prof. Babcock [of Boston University] stated that the stomach contained at least 45 grains of arsenic ... Dr. Terry, of Fall River, testified to analyzing the vest pocket of the deceased and finding arsenic therein, and also analyzing a stain on the carpet where deceased vomited some two weeks previous to his death, while his wife was absent from home. Arsenic was found in the stain. Evidence was also introduced to show that the deceased had for a week before his sickness talked about his dying."

Rosalie A. Thyng was arrested for murdering her husband by arsenic poisoning, with a trial date of May the following year.

THE TRIAL

John H. Thyng, George's brother, testified at trial that Mrs. Thyng had told him that she had a guilty conscience. William T. Freelove testified that he purchased 10 cents worth of arsenic for Rosalie two days before her husband's death. Mary E. Freelove, wife of William, according to the *Boston Post* (May 24, 1876), "testified to hearing Mrs. Thyng say that when the rope was around her neck she wouldn't die with a lie in her mouth, and that if people knew all they wouldn't blame her." Rosalie testified in her defense that none of this was true.

On the third day of the trial, evidence was introduced which impeached the story told by Mr. Freelove. The druggist that Freelove said sold him the arsenic testified that never happened.

OUTCOME

On May 27, 1876, Rosalie A. Thyng was acquitted. Writes the *Boston Post*, "The Court room rang with applause which was promptly checked by the Sheriff, and the prisoner, losing the listlessness which has characterized her throughout the trial, broke into violent sobs. The District Attorney announced that the Government had no further cause of action against her and she was discharged. She was surrounded by a large number of friends and the congratulations of the result of the trial were most hearty."

AFTERWORD

It is possible that George H. Thyng was what was known as an "arsenic eater"—a person who voluntarily consumed arsenic for its (believed) curative properties. Once consumed repeatedly, the user can become an addict, "When once they contract the habit of arsenic eating they remain slaves for life."

According to census records, Rosalie and George had two children, Cora D., born in 1874 and died in 1965, and George H., born 1875 and died in 1941. Another child was born to Rosalie after her husband's death: Walter S., born in 1879, and marked illegitimate on his birth record. All three children were given the last name of Thyng. Rosalie remarried on September 12, 1880, to Allen G. Hathaway, in Westport, Massachusetts. By 1900, Rosalie was widowed once again and living with her stepmother in Westport. She is also listed as a mother of only two living children. Rosalie died on November 5, 1932.

FURTHER READING

Kent, Dr. James Tyler. *The Medica of Homeopathic Remedies*. 1912
"Murder Trial." *Boston Post* (Boston, Massachusetts), May 24, 1876.
"Murder Trial at New Bedford." *Boston Post* (Boston, Massachusetts), May 25, 1876.
"Murder Trial." *Boston Post* (Boston, Massachusetts), May 26, 1876.
"Acquitted." *Boston Post* (Boston, Massachusetts), May 27, 1876.

DENNIS DUNN, INFANT

CRIME

Infanticide—baby thrown from the second floor tenement window of Six-and-a-Half Street, Fall River, Massachusetts, on July 24, 1876.

VICTIM

Dennis Dunn, 16 months

ACCUSED

Mary Ellen Dunn, mother, 35

DETAILS

Mrs. Dunn was a drunkard and had been brought to Court repeatedly for this charge. No one was surprised when she committed this dastardly deed on one of her children.

As reported in *The New York Times*, "Mrs. Ellen Dunn, of Fall River, Mass., in a drunken frenzy last evening threw her child, eighteen months old, from the third-story window, fatally injuring it."

The tenement was described in the *Victorian Vistas* as "disgusting ... with great pools of stagnant water, deep enough to drown a child in, its mud, garbage and filthy smells ... enough to sicken the passer-by."

Ellen's husband, John Dunn, was formerly a laborer who had recently left the city to find work in the Lake Superior Copper Mines in Michigan. The Dunns were the parents of five children: Michael, aged twelve, a boy of about 7 years of age, two girls, aged about 5 and 3, and infant Dennis, aged 16 months.

According to the *Fall River Daily Evening News* (July 25, 1876), John Dunn had "from time to time" sent back his wages to his family. His wife had received $10 the Friday before the murder, "a portion of the money appears to have been spent by the woman for rum." The oldest son, Michael, worked in the mills to help support the family.

According to Michael's testimony, as reported in the newspaper (July 27, 1876), "When mother was not in liquor she was as good as any mother could be. I never knew of her whipping any of the children, unless by scolding or a light slap, except me. ... She whipped me two or three Sundays ago. She was in liquor at the time."

On July 24, Mrs. Dunn told Michael that she was ill (she "had been on a drunken spree much of the time" since Friday). She sent Michael "to go get her some liquor, ten cents worth of whiskey." When the lad returned home, his mother drank half of the whiskey. He noted that "she was not very well in her senses" (*Fall River Daily Evening News*, July 27, 1876).

Young Dennis had been sick for about a month with whooping cough. All was well when Michael left the house around 3 p.m. About two hours later, Michael "saw officer Regan with [his] little sister on the street taking her home. [The policeman] went up with her and woke [Mrs. Dunn]," which "made her worse than she had been at any time during the day." Michael said he saw his mother at the window and she told him to come up stairs. He decided not to because he "was afraid ... as she looked wild. I was afraid she would whip me" (*Fall River Daily Evening News*, July 27, 1876).

As reported in *Parallel Lives*, "According to eyewitnesses, Mrs. Dunn had spent a portion of the afternoon 'drinking again,' becoming 'very noisy' and 'beating her children,' which attracted the attention of several neighbors, including Mrs. Olive Fish, who lived 'in the lower tenement of the same house,' and Nellie Driscoll, another Six-and-a-Half Street resident. According to Mrs. Fish, she 'went out to see what the matter was' and 'heard the neighbors say that Mrs. Dunn was killing her children.' Drawn by the goings-on in the third floor tenement, a crowd soon formed on the street, which attracted the attention of Nellie, who, when she 'went out and asked Mrs. Fish what the matter was,' received the appalling reply that 'Mrs. Dunn was killing her children.'"

Neighbors testified at Mrs. Dunn's trial that they had witnessed her beating the baby with a stick (about a foot and a half long), holding him up by his arm, dropping him on the floor, and striking him on his back. She was seen beating another of her children, returning shortly to abusing the infant.

From *Parallel Lives* we learn that "Nellie went

outside and 'stood looking up' at the window of the Dunn tenement, at which time she, to her horror, 'saw Mrs. D. take the child by the legs ... holding [him] out of the window.' Pleading, Nellie 'asked her not to kill the child,' at which point Mrs. Dunn 'struck it against the house two or three times and threw it into the street,' remarking, 'there's one, I'll give you another.' The child 'fell on the banister' and landed over twelve feet from the house. Frantically, Nellie Driscoll 'ran to catch the child, but it struck before [she] could get it.'"

Daniel Dunn was severely injured and lived for an addition forty-five minutes before he died, having suffered a great deal. The jury at the coroner's inquest ruled "that the boy ... came to his death at the hands of Ellen Dunn ... from excessive beating with a stick, a strip of board, and then being thrown by her from a window in the third story of the house ... to the ground" (*Fall River Daily Evening News*, July 27, 1876).

THE TRIAL

The trial of Ellen Dunn was held in September, 1876, at the Superior Court in Taunton, Massachusetts.

OUTCOME

While proven guilty for the act of killing Dennis Dunn, the jury determined that "they are not satisfied [Mrs. Dunn] was of sound mind when the act of killing was done, so as to be legally accountable" (*Commonwealth of Massachusetts vs. Ellen Dunn*). After a hearing on her mental condition, Ellen Dunn was discharged and released.

FURTHER READING

Commonwealth of Massachusetts vs. Ellen Dunn, Bristol County Superior Court, Docket #1258, September 14, 1876.

Martins, Michael and Dennis Binette. *Parallel Lives: A Social History of Lizzie A. Borden and Her Fall River*. Fall River Historical Society, 2010.

New York Times, July 25, 1876.

"No Indictment." *Fall River Daily Evening News*, September 15, 1876.

"Shocking Affair." *Fall River Daily Evening News*, July 25, 1876.

Silvia, Philip T., Jr., PhD. *Victorian Vistas: Fall River, 1865-1885*. Fall River: R.E. Smith Printing Co., 1987.

"The Case of Mrs. Dunn." *Fall River Weekly News*, August 3, 1876.

"The Child Murder." *Fall River Daily Evening News*, July 27, 1876.

GALLERY

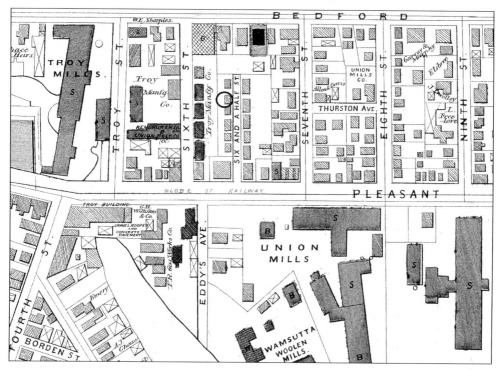

1883 atlas of Fall River. Six-and-a-Half Street, where the tragedy took place, is in the upper center of the image. The Dunn tenement building is circled. *Map courtesy of the State Library of Massachusetts.*

M. ALBERT SEABURY

CRIME	Murder in Little Compton, Rhode Island, by pitchfork, on the beach on December 2, 1882.
VICTIM	M. Albert Seabury, 53
ACCUSED	Edward "Ned" Davis, 37
DETAILS	

The abrasive elder M. Albert Seabury was found taking the then-valuable commodity of seaweed from the shoreline below his property for use on his farm as fertilizer. He claimed he had rights to do so but old deeds never proved it. Davis, the accused, was mild-mannered and claimed his innocence while other investigations into the killing began.

According to the *Hartford Courant*, "Albert Seabury, a well-to-do farmer residing near Seaconnet Beach [sic], in Little Compton, was found murdered on the beach yesterday morning. He had gone to the beach before breakfast, with his cart and oxen, to gather sea weed. His son went to look for him and found him dead on the sand, with the tide already within a few feet of him. His face was bruised, his jaw broken, and probably his neck broken."

According to *The Boston Weekly Globe* (December 5, 1882), the details of the circumstances, "as narrated by the family and neighbors, are as follows: Mr. Seabury started from his house at about 7 o'clock Saturday morning with a yoke of oxen and cart to get a load of seaweed from the shore ... About 9 o'clock, as he had not returned to breakfast, Mrs. Seabury sent her son [William], a lad 16 years of age, to see why his father had not returned. The boy went down to the beach and found his father lying dead upon the shore, the body still warm and the head and face covered with blood. The body was found on the west side of the creek; the ox team and cart, loaded with seaweed, were on the east side. The body when found was within ten feet of the water, and Willie dragged his father's body up from where it lay, beyond the reach of the tide. He then ran to the house of Mr. John S. Almy, about one-eighth of a mile distant, for assistance. By the time Mr. Almy arrived on the scene the tide had come in and washed away all traces of a struggle on the sand, if there had been one."

It was also reported that "for some time past there has been considerable hard feeling in regard to collecting seaweed on the shore of the Seaconet river [sic]. Forty years ago this question was brought before the courts, and the privilege was given to the abutters to claim all the seaweed above high water mark, and below that the privilege was granted to whoever might choose to gather it. The property on which Mr. Seabury was gathering seaweed belonging to a man named Ned Davis, and the family state that Mr. Davis has been heard to say that if he ever caught Seabury on his beach, one of them would have to be carried off the beach. Other expressions of the kind had been heard, and there was much ill-feeling between them. Davis was seen to leave the lane leading up from the beach to the main road by two persons about five or ten minutes before Willie Seabury started down the lane to look for his father. The house of Henry Almy is nearest the beach, but in going for assistance, the boy Willie passed his house and ran up to Thomas Almy's on the hill. Mr. Henry Almy was heard to say, as the neighbors were viewing the body, 'This is what comes of stealing seaweed'" (*The Boston Weekly Globe*, December 5, 1882).

Medical evidence determined that there were four blows across Seabury's face, "such as could be produced by a four-tined dung fork; that across the back of the head and neck was a wound which crushed the spinal cord, producing death; that such a wound could be produced by a blow from a round instrument, as the nadle of a fork; that a four-pronged dung fork—one which Seabury used—was found sticking in the sand, and lying partially across the body; that on the handle, a short distance from the shank, were two spots of blood, while at the shank were traces of blood as if partly rubbed off by seaweed and sand. This fork, the government claimed, was the weapon which produced death" (*The Boston Weekly Globe*, December 19, 1882).

THE TRIAL

The trial in Town Hall lasted from 10:30 a.m. to 6 p.m., with Atty. James M. Morton from Fall River for the defense and Nicholas Hathaway and John W. Cummings, Esq., the author's grandfather, representing the prosecution.

According to *The Boston Weekly Globe* (December 19, 1882), "a boy seated on a wall by the roadside about 8 o'clock that morning, testified to seeing Davis drive in a light wagon up the lane leading from the beach, turn into the road, and drive past him toward Little Compton commons. Davis admitted driving past the boy that morning, and seeing him sitting on the wall, but claimed that he drove out from his barn and not from the lane. Davis also claimed that, although he lived only the sixteenth of a mile from Seabury, and was his nearest neighbor, he did not hear of the murder until 2 o'clock Monday afternoon. He said he drove to Little Compton commons Saturday morning for his wife; returned home about noon; was at home Saturday afternoon, Sunday and Monday, and the first knowledge he had of the murder which had been for two days the talk of the town was Monday afternoon, when his mother-in-law, living nearly four miles from the scene, came to his house and told him Seabury had been found dead on the beach, and that he, Davis, was suspected of murdering him.

"Seabury's son testified that about a year ago Davis told him that if Seabury persisted in gathering seaweed on his beach some day one of them would be carried off the beach dead. Davis submitted his testimony that he had not spoken to Seabury for about a year owning to a quarrel about seaweed" (*The Boston Weekly Globe*, December 19, 1882).

OUTCOME

The evidence was not sufficient enough, according to the three trial justices, to send Davis to the Grand Jury and secure an indictment.

AFTERWORD

Davis was released but local folks wanted the investigation to continue but nothing was ever determined.

FURTHER READING

"A Farmer Murdered." *Hartford Courant* (Hartford, Connecticut), December 4, 1882.

"Davis Released." *The Boston Weekly Globe* (Boston, Massachusetts), December 19, 1882.

Lisle, Janet. *A History of Little Compton, A Home by the Sea, 1820-1850.* Little Compton Historical Society, 2012.

"The Little Compton Murder." *The Boston Weekly Globe* (Boston, Massachusetts), December 5, 1882.

GALLERY

"Seaweed" courtesy of the artist, Kyle E. Bartlett and the Little Compton Historical Society.

HERBERT L. HOXIE, INFANT

CRIME

Father of illegitimate male child accused of drowning him in the Acushnet River, in New Bedford, Massachusetts, on August 9, 1885.

VICTIM

Infant son, Herbert L. Hoxie, alias Herbert L. Woodward, 3 months

ACCUSED

Herbert J. Hoxie, 18

DETAILS

Herbert Hoxie was charged with tying a stone to the neck of his three-month-old illegitimate child and throwing it in the Acushnet River, where the body was found on August 14, and identified by its clothes.

According to the *Wilkes-Barre Times Leader* (November 4, 1886), "three boys found in the water, near the beach, on the south side of Crow Island, in this harbor [New Bedford], the dead body of an infant. Around its shoulders and under its arms was a cord, which fastened a stone weighing eight or ten points, to the little' one's breast, and it was evident that some one had sought to rid himself of the child in this inhuman manner. More than the usual interest was awakened in the case, as the child's clothing indicated that it had been well cared for. The medical examiner thought the infant was about three months old, and that it had been in the water about three weeks.

"A few weeks passed and as new clew was found the circumstance was nearly forgotten. About six weeks ago [the article is dated November 4, 1886] the catboat *Siria*, valued at $1,200, was stolen from Onset bay, and a few days after Deputy Sheriff Hurley, of Wareham, arrested Herbert J. Hoxie, a young man who had resided in this city, for the theft. Hoxie was found at Cuttyhunk with a young woman who claimed to be his wife and was taken to Wareham. He is now in confinement awaiting trial.

"Since Hoxie's arrest it is said that Deputy Sheriff Hurley has discovered facts connecting the young man with the drowning of the child. He is said to be the father, and after the crime, it is said, he told the young woman who now claims to be his wife that he had left the child on a doorstep, while he told his parents that he had sent it to friends in New York."

Hoxie had previously said he took the yacht to take his wife on a pleasure voyage to Florida. According to a report in the *Burlington Free Press*, "A child born to the Hoxies on September 3 was missed by the neighbors early last week. Suspicions of foul play were at once excited. It is learned today [October 7] that on the night of September 27, the parents left the child at the door of the Orphan Home in New Bedford." This was apparently a lie, as the child's body was discovered in August.

THE TRIAL

The trial was held in April of 1888. Very little reporting was done in the newspapers. On April 27, 1888, Herbert J. Hoxie was acquitted of the murder of his infant son. The jury returned its verdict after a day of deliberation.

FURTHER READING

Boston Weekly Globe (Boston, Massachusetts), May 2, 1888.
"Crime Will Leak Out." *Wilkes-Barre Times Leader* (Wilkes-Barre, Pennsylvania), November 4, 1886.
"For Murdering His Child." *Wilkes-Barre Times Leader* (Wilkes-Barre, Pennsylvania), April 24, 1888.
"Herbert J. Hoxie." *Boston Post* (Boston, Massachusetts), April 22, 1887.
"Hoxie Acquitted." *The Inter Ocean* (Chicago, Illinois), April 28, 1888.
"Staling [sic] a Yacht for His Wife." *The Burlington Free Press* (Burlington, Vermont), October 8, 1886.

PETER E. JOHNSON

CRIME

Hatchet murder of prominent Gay Head Indian, whose body was found in a boat that had run aground at Egg Island in New Bedford Harbor, New Bedford, Massachusetts, on June 9, 1891.

VICTIM

Peter E. Johnson, 45

ACCUSED

Charles J. Tighe, 29

DETAILS

Peter E. Johnson was found murdered in the bottom of a boat that was aground on Egg Island, in the Acushnet River, about a mile north of Fort Phoenix in Fairhaven, Massachusetts. According to a report in *The Times-Picayune*, "Joseph Hamel, a fisherman, was out in the river with George Frates about 8 o'clock. He was near the island when he was hailed by a man who wanted to be taken off to the mainland. Hamel said he didn't have time, and then the man offered $1.50 for the passage. Hamel accepted the offer and the man got aboard. Just as the boat reached the Fairhaven shore the stranger jumped over into the water and waded to dry land. Then he said he had no money, but had an uncle and a brother in the city who would pay. With this he disappeared behind Petticoat beacon, adding: 'Now you go back and look after my boat; I'll be back and pay you.'

"Hamel and Frates went back to the island and on going ashore they were horrified to find on the east side, opposite from where they took the stranger off, the body of a man lying near the boat, face down. Blood besmeared the boat from end to end, and a felt hat, which was also in the boat, was cut and had hair adhering to the edges. A pile of rope was covered with blood. Hamel did not stop for further investigation, but left for the mainland at once. The matter was at once reported to the Fairhaven authorities and Selectman John I. Bryant sent a constable to the island to look out for the body pending the arrival of the medical examiner.

"It has been learned that Johnson, a man named George Fletcher and a white man left this city at 7 o'clock last night in Johnson's boat. All these had been drinking, and a quart bottle of liquor was in the boat. This afternoon, after a description of the man who is supposed to have committed the murder was given out, several liquor dealers claim to have seen him in their saloons. That the murderer came to this city there can be no doubt, for W.B. Wood, pawnbroker, has a clue worth having. At about 1:30 a man came into his shop and wanted to trade his coat and hat for an old one to get a little money, he said, to get a meal. Wood noticed that the man had some dirt, as he supposed, on his clothes, and he told the man the clothing looked as if he had slept in a sewer. The man said he guessed it was only dirt that would brush off, and asked Wood for another coat and hat and 50 cents to boot. Wood told his clerk to give the man the money, which was done, the man giving the name of Charles Marston.

"After the news of the murder had reached the city, Wood noticed that the description of the man from whom he purchased the coat and hat exactly tallied with the description of the man who is supposed to have committed the murder, and a remark made by Marston that he had been down the river on a bit of a time, came to Wood, who immediately examined the coat. On the sleeves were found dark stains, and on the inside lining of the sleeves were found large quantities of blood stains which had not been washed out in the heavy soaking they had received. The hat also, on being closely examined, was found to be spotted with blood. The man left the shop at 1:30, and was not seen again as far as heard from. George Fletcher, who went off in the boat with Johnson and the supposed murderer, has not been seen to-day, and in all probability he was killed also and thrown overboard, as there is no way to reaching land from Egg Island without a boat.

"Johnson's body was brought to this city this afternoon. The head had eleven cuts, and the little finger of the left hand is completely severed, and the back of the right hand is cut as if the man threw up his hands as a protection from the cruel blows."

John Cross told the *Fitchburg Sentinel* (June 11, 1891) that robbery was most probably the motive for the murder of Johnson. "Cross was well acquainted with Johnson, and frequently took him to his house to sober off. Johnson was also wont to make his boat fast to the stern of Cross' boat.

"Last Saturday Johnson did so and came ashore to get gulls' some eggs from Cross. He was then sober, but had been drinking the night before. He said he had met a stranger to whom he took a liking, and who was going on his next trip with him. They had drunk together, and Johnson had told him all about his pension, for which he had lately passed an examination. Peter's description of the stranger, Cross says, tallies with that of the prisoner now held for the murder.

"Cross advised Johnson to keep away from strangers, as they invariably got Peter drunk, and especially if Peter got his pension money, as he expected to on Monday. About 8 o'clock Johnson went aboard his boat, and Sunday morning went to pull his lobster traps. Monday morning John Sylvia, a young man employed by Cross, met Johnson off Black rock, rowing toward the city. When asked what his hurry was, he replied that he must be in the city at 10 o'clock to get his pension money.

"Mr. Cross thinks Johnson may have tried to draw his pension money, and then put to sea without having been successful, and that his new-made acquaintance killed him in the hope of getting the cash."

Charles Marston turned out to be Charles Tighe. In his defense, he claimed that while he did go off in the catboat with the two men, he had gone to sleep after much drink in the cuddy of the boat. The last thing he said he remembered was that the two Indians quarreled. He fell asleep again and when he woke up he found himself alone on Egg Island, with the boat high and dry. He said the blood on his coat came from the blood on the boat. He maintained his innocence and pleaded not guilty. He was held over until trial without bail.

Peter E. Johnson, a member of the Wampanoag Tribe

of Gay Head (Aquinnah), had figured prominently in an heroic event known as the *City of Columbus* disaster, which ran aground on Devil's Bridge off the Gay Head Cliffs in the early morning hours of January 18, 1884.

Charles Tighe was the son of Cornelius Tighe, a prominent businessman from Lawrence, Massachusetts. According to *The Wilkes-Barre Record* (June 20, 1891), Charles "married at 21, and six years later deserted his wife and two children for Clara Bell Gifford, wife of George Gifford, of New Bedford, a professional clairvoyant, who had left her husband. Tighe has frequently been under arrest on various charges and has served short terms in jail on Deer Island."

George Fletcher's body was never found. According to the *Fitchburg Sentinel* (June 11, 1891), "Fletcher sent word to his wife Monday afternoon that he would return home Wednesday morning, but he has not kept his word ... John Cross ... says that there is a basin in Priest's cove, and that if Fletcher is murdered his body will probably be found there, as that is where the tide would leave it. He says he thinks the murder was committed further south, and that the murderer, being unable to manage the boat, allowed her to drift on to Egg Island."

"Another theory advanced is that the murderer must first have disposed of Fletcher, and then, tackling Johnson, found him no easy victim. The cuts on Johnson's hands are explained in the belief that the Gay Header must have been pushed overboard, and while clinging to the gunwale of the boat was hacked ... Monday afternoon, J.K. Nye saw a colored man answering the description of Fletcher, washing out some part of his clothing in a pool by the side of the road in Westport. He thought it strange at the time. The man may possibly have been Fletcher bound to Fall River and then to New York" (*Fitchburg Sentinel*, June 11, 1891).

The next day, the same newspaper (June 13, 1891) reported that an oar was found by a patrolman who thought it looked like it was from a large boat. "The large oar generally carried in that boat is missing, and it is thought that Fletcher might have floated to ashore on it, the wind being right. Yesterday Charles Hall, a resident of Fairhaven, saw a negro skulking at the edge of some woods. When the latter saw that he was observed he hurried out of sight. Another resident of Fairhaven recalls to mind that he saw a colored man early Tuesday morning at the railroad crossing in that town. The description given by the lady resembles a description of Fletcher."

They continue, "Mrs. Fletcher is worried with the frequent visits made to her by reporters, and says that the theory advanced that her husband is the real murderer is all put up to get the white man off. She is sure her husband was drowned or murdered, having had a dream to that effect."

THE TRIAL

The trial was held in New Bedford in October. Tighe maintained his innocence.

OUTCOME

After deliberating for eighteen and a half hours, the jury adjudged Charles Tighe guilty of manslaughter. According to the *Essex County Herald*, "the prisoner manifested more uneasiness than at any previous time during the trial when informed that the jury had agreed. He turned deathly white, and regained his color only after a long and whispered consultation with his counsel ... it is claimed that one of the strongest circumstances, which made a decided impression upon the jury, was the finding of a spatter of blood in the right ear of the accused ... [which] led to the supposition that the fatal blows were dealt on the right hand. This, coupled with the fact that the right sleeves of both shirts were missing, did more in convicting Tighe than all other testimony together."

Charles J. Tighe was sentenced to seven years in state prison, with one day in solitary confinement.

ADDENDUM

According to the gripping story retold in Irving King's book on the Coast Guard, the wreck of the *City of Columbus* was a tragedy. On January 17, 1884 the steamer *City of Columbus* left Boston with 87 passengers and a crew of 45 under the command of Captain Schuler E. Wright. The captain went below to sleep, leaving the ship in the hands of his Second Mate. At 3:45 a.m., a lookout yelled that the Devil's Bridge buoy was off the port bow instead of starboard. Just then, the ship struck a double ledge of submerged rocks. The Second Mate ordered the *City of Columbus* to go port and Captain Wright ordered her to hard port. This caused the *City of Columbus* to smack against the reef. Wright tried to use sail but it only pushed the ship further onto the reef. Wright then decided to go over the reef, which proved to be fatal. He gathered the passenger and while explaining the situation to them, they were forced to the top deck when a rush of water came into the cabin. Once on deck, a giant wave struck and swept them into the frozen waters.

Lifeboats were useless, as the waves smashed them against the iron ship. Holding onto rigging and anything that would float, passengers and crew attempted to stay afloat in the rough seas. The lighthouse keeper and group of Gay Head Wampanoag Indians attempted to save as many people as could fit into two lifeboats. Those who dove off the rigging and swam to the lifeboats were saved.

The Revenue Cutter *Dexter* came to the rescue as well, and they were able to move about the wreckage and pull survivors off the rigging because their boat was much smaller. Only 17 crew members and 12 passengers survived the ordeal.

FURTHER READING

"Butchered a Hero." *Harrisburg Daily Independent* (Harrisburg, Pennsylvania), June 10, 1891.

"Charles Tighe Guilty of Manslaughter." *The Burlington Free Press* (Burlington, Vermont), October 24, 1891.

"The Egg Island Mystery." *Fitchburg Sentinel* (Fitchburg, Massachusetts), June 11, 1891.

"The Egg Island Tragedy." *Fitchburg Sentinel* (Fitchburg, Massachusetts), June 13, 1891.

"His Name is Charles Tighe." *The Wilkes-Barre Record* (Wilkes-Barre, Pennsylvania), June 20, 1891.

"Found Guilty of Manslaughter." *The Wilkes-Barre Record* (Wilkes-Barre, Pennsylvania), October 24, 1891.

"Johnson Dead in His Boat." *The Sun* (New York, New York), June 10, 1891.

"Johnson's Murderer." *The Cincinnati Enquirer* (Cincinnati, Ohio), June 21, 1891.

King, Irving H. *The Coast Guard Expands, 1865 - 1915: New Roles, New Frontiers.* Annapolis, MD: Naval Institute Press, 1996.

"A Life Saver Murdered." *The Boston Weekly Globe* (Boston, Massachusetts), June 16, 1891.

"Manslaughter the Verdict." *Essex County Herald* (Guildhall, Vermont), October 30, 1891.

"A Most Brutal Murder." *Fitchburg Sentinel* (Fitchburg, Massachusetts(, June 10, 1891.

"The Murdered Gay Head Indian." *The Sun* (New York, New York), June 11, 1891.

"Murdered on Egg Island." *The Times-Picayune* (New Orleans, Louisiana), June 19, 1891.

"Tighe Sentences to State Prison for Seven Years." *Fitchburg Sentinel* (Fitchburg, Massachusetts), October 31, 1891.

GALLERY

SS City of Columbus and Revenue Cutter *Dexter*, Shell and Hogan, 1884.

MARY TALLON

CRIME	Death following an abortion in Somerset, Massachusetts, November 9, 1891.
VICTIM	Mary Tallon, 22
ACCUSED	Dr. Thomas Shirley Vose, 48

DETAILS

Mary Tallon, who only spoke French, was married to Henry Tallon, but he left her the day after they were married. She was supported only by her own means as a domestic. Previously pregnant, she had two prior successful abortions by Dr. Vose in South Somerset.

Mary was described, in a news report in the *Philadelphia Inquirer*, as "the prettiest girl of the mills. ... Her beauty made her an object of general attraction ... having a rich complexion, with a wonderful head of golden hair and large hazel eyes."

According to *Parallel Lives*, Mary, a native of Canada, "was born Mary Marcheterre, the daughter of Michael and Mary Marcheterre, and had immigrated to America, settling in Fall River where she found work in the textile mills. On August 23, 1889, the twenty-two-year-old Mary and Henry Tallon, a man two years her junior, employed as a card grinder in a Fall River mill, were joined in marriage by Reverend Jacques Bellemare, associate pastor of St. Anne's Church. ... Alone, and with no means of support other than those of her own labor, she made the decision to terminate her pregnancy, and she knew of a physician willing to perform the procedure. [Her friend Henry Berube] escorted her to the South Somerset residence, on what was to be a fatal trip. It was not the first time he had assisted her in visiting Dr. Vose, the previous occasions being 'last August,' when he 'took her there twice.' During the October, 1891, visit, Berube stated that Dr. Vose advised his patient that 'she would be in a great deal of pain,' to which Mary replied that 'it would not be worse than it was the other time.'"

Mary had arrived for the abortion in mid-October. She was still at Dr. Vose's residence two weeks later when she died. According to the *Fall River Daily Globe*, on November 4, Dr. Vose sought the advice of Dr. Thomas A. Capen, and asked him to come to his house to see Tallon, who he said was suffering from "nothing more than a little rheumatism." Capen, however, discovered "a deplorable sight ... Lying there on an improvised bed [in the attic] was the body of a woman. She was suffering from a violent inflammation of the stomach and her pulse and temperature were far above normal." He said that her condition was grave and hopeless. Mary died soon after.

Vose then attempted to have Mary Tallon buried and told the undertaker that she had died of typhoid fever, so time was of the essence. After the police became involved, on the report of two unidentified informants that a woman had died under suspicious circumstances in his house, Mary Tallon was taken to the medical examiner for an autopsy.

It is important to note that, according to *Parallel Lives*, "Throughout the nineteenth century, abortion was widely practiced, constituting, for many women, the only viable means of birth control. ... At the beginning the century, no state laws existed in opposition to abortion, as it was commonly believed that the procedure, prior to 'quickening,' the term used for the first movement of the fetus, was not criminal."

Since her death was ruled as having been caused by the procedure, Dr. Vose was arrested "on a charge of being criminally connected with the death of Mary Tallon."

THE TRIAL

Dr. Vose was arrested and put on trial in November of 1892 for using a certain instrument in the body to procure a miscarriage that resulted in death. On December 2, the jury found him guilty.

OUTCOME

Dr. Vose was sentenced to five years at hard labor and one day in solitary confinement at the State Prison in Charlestown, Massachusetts.

AFTERWORD

In January, 1894, Dr. Vose was sent from jail in Boston to a lunatic hospital in Worcester where he remained until his death on April 5, 1894, of "secondary dementia and exhaustion."

FURTHER READING

"Court Chronicles." *Fall River Daily Globe*, November 16, 1891.
"A Serious Charge." *Fall River Daily Evening News*, November 10, 1891.
Martins, Michael and Dennis Binette. *Parallel Lives: A Social History of Lizzie A. Borden and Her Fall River*. Fall River Historical Society, 2010.
"Sad End of a Factory Belle." *Philadelphia Inquirer* (Philadelphia, Pennsylvania), November 12, 1891.

ANDREW AND ABBY BORDEN

CRIME

The unsolved hatchet murders of Andrew and Abby Borden in their home at 92 Second Street, Fall River, Massachusetts, on August 4, 1892.

VICTIMS

Andrew Jackson Borden and Abby Durfee Gray Borden, 70 and 64

ACCUSED

Lizzie Andrew Borden, 32, daughter of Andrew Borden

DETAILS

It is very difficult to construct an accurate retelling the murder of Andrew and Abby Borden. Numerous authors have done their best to describe the events of that morning, mostly framing their telling from an assumption of guilt of one of the characters. According to Borden expert, Stefani Koorey, "One of the problems with this enigmatic case is that the time lines of those involved (where they were before, during, and after the crimes) are inconsistent within themselves and in comparison to other's versions of events. Famous for her contrary explanations, Lizzie Borden, in her inquest testimony, offered up differing accounts of her whereabouts that fateful morning. While her contradictory answers may be due to stress and the doses of morphine she had been given to calm her nerves by family physician Dr. Seabury Bowen, her inability to remember properly where she was and exactly what she was doing has been the subject of debate for over a century."

That being said, we can be sure of only these facts. That on Thursday morning, August 4, 1892, a person or persons unknown, at approximately 9:30 a.m., killed Abby Borden in the second floor guest room with a hatchet, striking her 19 times about the head. Ninety minutes later, at approximately 11 a.m., Andrew Borden was likewise felled by eleven hatchet blows to his head as he was resting on the sofa in the first floor sitting room. The only other persons who were present in and about the house during those hours were the 32-year-old daughter of Andrew Borden, Lizzie, and the family maid, Bridget Sullivan, who was in and out of house as she washed the windows. Emma Borden, Lizzie's older sister by nine years, was away visiting friends in Fairhaven, Massachusetts.

The police quickly focused on Lizzie as the main suspect because her behavior was judged to be curious—she remained calm (did not cry or become hysterical as they expected she might) and famously replied to a question regarding the murder of her "mother" Abby Borden, "She is not my mother. She is my step-mother."

The murders of Andrew and Abby Borden occurred in an era before fingerprint technology became an established method of police investigation. By today's standards of forensic science, the police work in the Borden murders seems crude, sloppy, and disorganized. The evidence that remains for us to examine comes from various sources—primary source documents (Inquest, Preliminary Hearing, and Trial) as well as collections of artifacts in private and non-profit sources.

The Fall River Historical Society has the largest collection of resources from the case, including photographs, letters, personal papers, Abby's hair switch, the "handleless hatchet" (presented at trial as the possible murder weapon), and the bloody quilt and pillow shams from the guest room where Abby Borden was killed.

The supposed "crime scene photographs" are misnamed. These images were taken by a police photographer at approximately 3 p.m.—some four to five hours after the crimes. As such, these images must be viewed with skepticism. They are merely location shots of the placement of the bodies at the time of the crimes, with both Andrew and Abby having been moved by many doctors and policemen soon after their deaths. The bodies were returned to their assumed positions, with care taken to arrange their clothing and shoes for the sake of propriety.

Lizzie Borden testified at the Inquest (held August 9 to 11, 1892) without the benefit of counsel, even though a warrant had been issued for her arrest on August 8 but had not been served. Because of this fact, her inquest testimony was ruled inadmissible at trial.

Lizzie was arraigned on August 12, plead not guilty and sent to Taunton, Massachusetts, to await the next stages of her legal ordeal. A Preliminary Hearing was held on August 25 to September 1 and the Grand Jury heard evidence in this case (among others) from November 7 to 21. Because Lizzie and Emma's friend, Alice Russell, approached the police to inform them that she had witnessed Lizzie burn a dress in the stove in the kitchen on Sunday after the murders, the Grand Jury was reconvened on December 1, and Russell testified to what she saw. Because of this, it is believed, an indictment was handed down charging Lizzie Borden with the murder of Andrew and Abby Borden. She was arraigned on May 8, 1893, in the Superior Court in New Bedford.

THE TRIAL

The "Trial of the Century," with Lizzie as the accused, took place before an all male jury in New Bedford, Massachusetts, in June of 1893. Former Massachusetts Governor George D. Robinson, Andrew J. Jennings, and Melvin O. Adams represented Lizzie and were considered by modern scholars as a "dream team." The prosecutor for the Commonwealth was William H. Moody, a future United States Attorney General and Associate Justice of the Supreme Court, and great uncle of the authors' friend, Michael Moody.

The trial lasted from June 5 to June 20. The prosecution asserted that Lizzie Borden was the killer and her motive was financial. There was no eyewitness testimony and all evidence was circumstantial. Lizzie was never seen with blood on her, even though she called for Bridget to "come quick, someone has killed Father" moments after the last crime and appeared clean and dry. Testimony from a druggist at Smith's Drug Store that Lizzie Borden had attempted to purchase prussic acid (to reportedly clean her sealskin cape) the day before the murders was not allowed in court.

The jury deliberated barely one hour and returned a verdict of not guilty.

OUTCOME

There was no sentencing as Lizzie Borden was acquitted of the crimes.

AFTERWORD

Lizzie and Emma Borden purchased 7 French Street (now 306) in the Lower Highland area of Fall River in 1893 and Lizzie lived there until her death in 1927. Emma left the house and her sister in 1905. Emma died in Newmarket, New Hampshire, nine days after her sister, Lizzie.

The enduring doggerel/skip-rope rhyme continues to be recited over one hundred years later, even though the facts of the case are not in the least represented by the poem:

> "Lizzie Borden took an axe
> And gave her mother forty whacks.
> When she saw what she had done
> She gave her father forty-one."

Periodically, at evening dinner at 283 Prospect Street in the Highland Section of Fall River, Massachusetts, nearly sixty years after the event, Attorney John B. Cummings, son of former Mayor Attorney John W. Cummings, would relate to his wife and son, the author of this book, the former mayor's feelings about the event. Cummings Sr. was contacted in England shortly after the murders took place and asked to serve as counsel for the accused, but since he did not believe in her innocence neither the elder Cummings, the first Irish Catholic Mayor in the city's history, nor any member of his law firm would agree to represent her. They did however, represent Bridget Sullivan, the Irish maid.

FURTHER READING

Chapman, Sherry. *Lizzie Borden: Resurrections: A History of the People Surrounding the Borden Case Before, During, and After the Trial.* PearTree Press, 2014.

Commonwealth of Massachusetts VS. Lizzie A. Borden; The Knowlton Papers, 1892-1893. Eds. Michael Martins and Dennis A. Binette. Fall River, MA: Fall River Historical Society, 1994.

Conforti, Joseph A. *Lizzie Borden on Trial: Murder, Ethnicity, and Gender.* University of Kansas Press, 2015.

Geary, Rick. *The Borden Tragedy.* New York: NBM Publishing, 1997.

LizzieAndrewBorden.com

Martins, Michael and Dennis Binette. *Parallel Lives: A Social History of Lizzie A. Borden and Her Fall River.* Fall River Historical Society, 2010.

Miller, Sarah. *The Borden Murders: Lizzie Borden and the Trial of the Century.* New York: Schwartz & Wade, 2016.

"Nothing in Annals of Fall River Attracted As Much Attention as Borden Murder Case," *Fall River Herald News* (Fall River, Massachusetts), September 19, 1958.

Pearson, Edmund. *The Trial of Lizzie Borden.* New York: Doubleday, 1937. Rpt. as The Trial of Lizzie Borden by Edmund Pearson; Notable Trials Library Edition, Foreword by Alan Dershowitz. Delran, NJ: Gryphon, 1991.

Porter, Edwin H. *The Fall River Tragedy.* Fall River, MA: George R. H. Buffinton, Press of J. D. Munroe, 1893. Rpt. with new introduction by Robert Flynn. Portland, ME: King Philip Pub., 1985.

Radin, Edward D. *Lizzie Borden: The Untold Story.* NY: Simon and Schuster, 1961.

Rebello, Leonard. *Lizzie Borden: Past and Present.* Al-Zach Press, 1999.

GALLERY

Lizzie Andrew Borden. *Boston Globe,* August 8, 1892.

92 Second Street. *Boston Globe*, June 26, 1893.

Left: Andrew J. Borden as he was known in life. *Right:* Andrew J. Borden as he was found on August 4, 1892. *Boston Globe*, August 5 and 6, 1892.

Abby Borden as she lay after death. *Boston Globe*, August 5, 1892.

The Borden Jury. *Image courtesy of a private collection.*

"Only picture of Miss Borden taken since her arrest on the charge of Murder."
Boston Globe, June 12, 1893.

BERTHA M. MANCHESTER

CRIME

Axe murder on May 31, 1893, on the Manchester farm in the north end of Fall River, Massachusetts.

VICTIM

Bertha M. Manchester, 22

ACCUSED

Jose Correa deMello, 18

DETAILS

Bertha M. Manchester, 22, daughter of Stephen C. Manchester, was hacked to death with an axe in the early afternoon of Memorial Day, 1893, at the Manchester milk farm on upper New Boston Road (now Meridian Street), in Fall River, Massachusetts. Bertha's murder occurred just five days before the start of the Lizzie Borden trial and, because of this and the similar nature of the crime, created a national interest in the case.

According to *The Times* of Philadelphia, Bertha "was last seen alive around 7:30 o'clock this morning when her father, Stephen Manchester, left for this city, accompanied by his son and hired boy, to deliver milk on his regular route. About 2 o'clock this afternoon they arrived home. Freddie, his 12-year-old boy, ran ahead to the house to get something to eat. He opened the kitchen door and saw his murdered sister laying in a pool of blood on the floor. He ran back to the barn and told his father, who immediately notified the police. A hasty examination was made by the officers of the house and its immediate surroundings. A bloody axe was found in a wood pile near the back fence.

"The examination of the body disclosed horrible conditions. The young girl was lying close to the foot of the stove. Her right leg was drawn under the body, her clothes were partially drawn from her hips and her head and face were frightfully mutilated. There were four long deep cuts on the back of the head and the top of the skull was crushed to a jelly. There were several cuts to the face and nose and two of the girl's teeth were found on the floor beside her. Her loose hair was matted with blood and her arms and face were covered with it.

"On searching the house the police found that the girl's bed room had been rifled of some of its contents. This leads the police to believe that the motive of the awful butchery was robbery."

Other newspaper reports focused on the unhappy family life of poor Bertha. According to the *Brooklyn Daily Eagle* (May 31, 1893), "persons who know the murdered girl say she has been a household drudge the past four years. Her father married his second wife about eight years ago, but they did not live happily together, although a boy [Frederick] was born to them. For many months the woman has been drawing a current sum for her maintenance, while her husband has been endeavoring to obtain a divorce. There are many stories of the girl's life cropping out, which seemed most incredible when her youth and physique are considered. It is known that for many months she has been her father's greatest help in caring for his nineteen cows, three horses and large farm house. She had frequently complained of her hard lot in life. ... All speak of [Bertha] as modest, retiring, self-sacrificing. ... She possessed a good figure and face, and was attractive and lovable."

Medical Examiner William A. Dolen determined that Bertha had died around 9:30 in the morning.

On June 4, Jose Correa deMello, a Portuguese immigrant from the Azores, was arrested for the murder and arraigned the following morning. According to the *Middletown Times Press*, "On the day of the murder [Correa deMello] entered a French Canadian shoe dealers' store near the south end of Sagamore Mill and asked in broken English for a pair of shoes. He pulled out of his pocket a silver trade dollar, bright and apparently new. He also pulled out from his pocket a silver half dollar with a hole in it. [It was] learned that Mr. Manchester had given silver trade dollars to Bertha ... Bertha's trade dollar was kept in her bureau drawer, and in the drawer with it the officers learned there was also kept a half dollar with a hole it in. ... During the investigation Carreiro [sic] denied he had ever offered a silver half dollar with a hole in it to the dealer or that he had any conversation with the shoe dealer in relation to the trade dollar. A Portuguese

86   *Murder, Manslaughter, and Mayhem on the SouthCoast*

across the river, who acted as interpreter with the French Canadian shoe dealer, stated positively that Carreiro [sic] had offered a half dollar with a hole in it and that there was a discussion about the value of the trade dollar.

"The shoe dealer said that Carreiro[sic] had what appeared to be a lady's pocketbook with a clasp on it, and that he took money from it. Carreiro [sic] denies that he ever had a pocketbook. None was found in his possession. Her pocketbook was taken from Bertha's room."

Additional, they reported that "Marshal [Rufus] Hilliard said that Carreiro [sic] had told a number of very conflicting stories since he was brought in. He also said that there were no scratches to be found on his face. Carreiro [sic] had been in this city only six or eight months. In that time he had worked in several places and had acquired the reputation of a shiftless, worthless sort of fellow. He is 21 or 22 years of age and has a moustache and goatee."

The *Philadelphia Inquirer* notes that "On the night of June 6 police officers drove the prisoner to a point near Highland road, less than a mile northwest of the Manchester home. The police were led by the handcuffed Correiro [sic] into a meadow near by, and after a few moments' search in the farm wall, Correiro [sic] pulled out Bertha's watch and gave it up. Correiro [sic] went to the Manchester house to rob it, and entered it, not by the back door, but the south entrance to the kitchen. He knew the habits of the old man, and fixed his visit at a time when Bertha Manchester must be alone. After taking the watch and money he came down stairs, only to find the daughter, ax in hand. She had undoubtedly heard the intruder as he worked in the pantry, and had grabbed the weapon that afterward caused her death, because it was the most handy thing to protect herself with. She met Correiro [sic] at the entrance to the dining room, he having finished the search in the rooms above. He struck the ax as if to ward off a blow, and the blade made the peculiar cut afterward found in the girl's forehead. He struck her in the mouth as she grappled him, and this blow perhaps knocked out the teeth that were afterward found. Correiro [sic] was recognized, and he felt that in order to get away he must kill, and he did."

THE TRIAL

The accused, who spoke no English, plead not guilty at his arraignment but changed the plea to guilty on September 18. He was convicted of second-degree murder on January 8, 1894.

OUTCOME

Jose Correa deMello was sentenced to state prison for life.

AFTERWORD

Twenty years later, on December 31, 1913, Jose Correa deMello was pardoned from any further imprisonment under the condition that if he committed any crime he would be returned to jail for the remainder of his term. Upon release, he was sent back to his native Azores and directed never return to the United States.

FURTHER READING

"Bertha Manchester's Slayer." *Scranton Republican* (Scranton, Pennsylvania), June 19, 1893.

"Fall River Mystery." *The Evening Star* (Washington, D.C.), June 17, 1893.

"Fall River's Fiend." *St. Louis Post Dispatch*, June 2, 1893.

"Fall River's New Mystery." *The Evening World* (New York, New York), May 31, 1893.

"Little Doubt of Guilt." *Brooklyn Daily Eagle* (Brooklyn, New York), June 17, 1893.

"How He Killed the Girl." *Philadelphia Inquirer* (Philadelphia, Pennsylvania), June 18, 1893.

"Like the Borden Murders." *The Sun* (New York, New York), May 31, 1893.

Martins, Michael and Dennis Binette. *Parallel Lives: A Social History of Lizzie A. Borden and Her Fall River*. Fall River Historical Society, 2010.

"Miss Manchester's Murder." *The Evening World* (New York, New York), June 17, 1893.

MurderByGaslight.com

"Murder Near Fall River." *Brooklyn Daily Eagle* (Brooklyn, New York), May 31, 1893.

"Murdered with an Axe." *The Times* (Philadelphia, Pennsylvania), May 31, 1893

"Northing in Annals of Fall River Attracted As Much Attention as Borden Murder Case," *Fall River Herald News* (Fall River, Massachusetts), September 19, 1958.

Phillips, Arthur Sherman. *Phillips History of Fall River. Fascicle III*. Fall River, Dover Press, 1946.

"Startling Parallelisms." *Boston Globe* (Boston, Massachusetts), June 1, 1893.

"Traced By the Coins." *Middletown Times Express* (Middletown, New York), June 5, 1893.

GALLERY

BERTHA MANCHESTER.

STEPHEN MANCHESTER.

Boston Globe, June 1, 1893.

Boston Globe, June 1, 1893.

Bertha Manchester grave at Oak Grove Cemetery. *Photo courtesy of Stefani Koorey.*

MARY ROBERTSON

CRIME	Husband stabbed wife to death in New Bedford, Massachusetts, on September 9, 1893.
VICTIM	Mary Robertson, 48
ACCUSED	Daniel M. Robertson, 45
DETAILS	

Daniel Robertson had been arrested for drunkenness in August, pleaded guilty, was fined $10, and put on probation until September 30 of the next year. Since he had only half of the funds necessary to pay the fine, he was kept in jail until September 9, 1893. Upon release, he went to his wife's boarding house to get the funds. Mary Robertson had sought a divorce from her husband while he was in jail but it was denied.

Reports *The Fitchburg Sentinel* (September 11, 1893), "At 1:30 he went to the front door and rang the bell. Mrs. Robertson refused to open the door for him. 'I must come in to get a change of clothing,' said Robertson, and his wife finally consented to open the door for him. The door was accordingly opened and Robertson went up stairs. Mrs. Robertson stopped to again lock the door. Both man and wife proceeded to the kitchen. Here they became engaged in another dispute. Robertson angrily demanded that his wife furnish him with some dinner. This she persistently refused to do. 'You shall give me my dinner,' exclaimed the irate man. Then the whole house, in fact the whole neighborhood, was aroused by two long, heartrending cries. [These] brought the young daughter Helen [age 16] to the scene. With blood pouring form two wounds on her forehead and cheek, her mother stood screaming for help. Over her stood her father, holding his wife by the hair and in his uplifted hand the blood covered knife. Miss Robertson screamed, and grabbing her father, made him give up the death dealing knife. Mrs. Robertson succeeded in getting away from the frenzied man and ran down the front stairs, as if to escape from the house.

"At the same time Robertson made his escape. Mrs. Robertson succeeded in reaching and opening the front door. About this time Dr. Fales, who was passing along the avenue, heard the woman's cries for help, and running to the open door found the woman bleeding and dying on the stairway. He picked the dying woman up and carried her to the dining room above. The woman was nearly dead when picked up, and in a few minutes after she was carried up stairs. She breathed her last breath.

"An examination of the wounds disclosed the fact that the woman had been stabbed twice. A ragged cut was made in the forehead just above the right eye. This wound was not deep and only penetrated to the bone. In the left cheek, just below the roof of the mouth. The facial artery was severed by the cut, and this was the direct cause of death. When the police arrived they found the deadly weapon on the floor of the kitchen, and this was immediately given into possession of the chief. The knife was an ordinary case knife with a black wood handle, and the blade was round and not very sharp."

The autopsy revealed that Mary Robertson had sustained four wounds. *The Evening Standard* (September 11, 1893) reported that "one was a long cut on the left arm, and the other was just above the right breast, the last named being quite deep ... Death resulted from hemorrhage of the small blood vessels of the sphemo-moxilliary pessa, which are behind the upper jaw and below the base of the skull."

According to *The Evening Standard* (September 11, 1893), "Robertson's career as a criminal has been extensive. May 14, 1890 he was fined $5 and costs for drunkenness. December 14, 1891 he was before the court for the same offense, but his case was continued. May 31, 1892, he received a sentence for larceny of a book which he pawned for rum. May 16th, this year, he was sentenced to three months in the house of correction for drunkenness, and on August 12 he was in default of payment of $10 for a similar offense. He has given the police considerable trouble at intervals for a period of years. Sixteen years ago when the daughter, his only child, was an infant in his arms, he was arrested for the theft of money from his wife. Officer James W. Arnett had just joined the police force, and the apprehension of Robertson was his first arrest."

THE TRIAL

According to *The Evening Standard* (September 11, 1893), who covered the trial in detail, Robertson was described thusly: "He has dark brown hair, and eyes of the same color, deeply sunken, and with overhanging brows. His forehead is wrinkled and between the eyes is a deep crease. His pose is thin and rather prominent, his face long and cheeks sunken, his chin square and determined, and his mouth is covered with a reddish-brown mustache. His face is covered with a rough stubble, and neither beard, mustache nor his hair show any signs of gray. He was dressed in an old suit of black clothes, the coat being a cutaway and the bosom of his white shirt appeared dirty. He wore no collar."

When asked to plead, Robertson refused, so a plea of not guilty was entered.

Officer James Arnett said that he spoke with Robertson in his jail cell at the Central station after he had been fined $10 for drunkenness. Robertson had only half the amount he needed. According to the *Boston Post* (March 8, 1894) "Arnett asked him if his wife wouldn't pay the fine, and Robertson replied that she was the cause of him being locked up. But he threatened to get square with her, telling the officer he would kill her. Robertson was not drunk at the time." Another witness testified that he had heard Robertson say, "She'd have paid my fine in court only a boarder told her not to. She's seeking a divorce from me but she didn't get it, and if she doesn't pay me out, I'll kill her when I get out." James Colbett, who was arrested and released with Robertson that day testified that "On the morning we came out of jail I asked Robertson if he was going to do the desperate deed he had said he was going to, and he said 'yes,' so I said I would not go along with him." More than half a dozen witnesses testified that Robertson threatened to kill his wife if she did not give him the money.

The defense argued that Robertson was drunk when the crime occurred and that it was a crime of passion, and thus not premeditated. In addition, Lawyer L. Le B. Holmes asked for pity on Robertson saying, according to the *Boston Post* (March 8, 1894), "I can remember a trial here a few months ago when a woman of great wealth was in the prisoner's place. A far different spectacle was then presented; flowers and gifts poured in from distinguished friends from far and near. I doubt not that in the eye of infinite pity his condition is just as dear as the condition of that woman." This was a reference to Lizzie Borden, who, in 1893, was acquitted in the same courtroom for the murder of Andrew and Abby Borden.

OUTCOME After deliberating two and a half hours, the jury found Daniel M. Robertson guilty of first degree murder and at a later court date was sentenced to death by hanging. Governor Frederic T. Greenhalge declined to commute the sentence of death. On December 14, 1894, Robertson was brought to the gallows in front of a few ticketed spectators. According to the *Springfield Republican*, what followed was a "sickening spectacle."

At 10:10 a.m., "the sheriff pulled the lock ... the gates fell and Robertson shot through the aperture at a terrific rate and fell to the floor with a dull thud, the rope having broken. The doomed man was picked up unconscious and blood trickling down his neck. He was carried to the trap and a new rope adjusted around his neck. He regained consciousness and again the gates swang ajar. This time, however, the murderer neck was broken by the drop of eight feet and he was cut down after hanging twelve minutes" (*The Bremen Enquirer*).

AFTERWORD Robertson's counsel was Timothy W. Coakley of Boston, who was the senior council in the Tighe murder case. The Tighe case was the last capital case tried in New Bedford with the exception of the Borden trial.

FURTHER READING

"Coakley Will Defend Robertson." *Boston Post* (Boston, Massachusetts), October 17, 1893.
The Evening Standard (New Bedford, Massachusetts), August 12, 1893.

"On the Gallows." *The Bremen Enquirer* (Bremen, Indiana), December 21, 1894.

"May Hang." *The Evening Standard* (New Bedford, Massachusetts), September 11, 1893.

"Refused to Commute Sentence." *Bangor Daily Whig and Courier* (Bangor, Maine), December 10, 1894.

"Robertson's Case Continued." *The Fitchburg Sentinel* (Fitchburg, Massachusetts), September 12, 1893.

"Show Premeditation." *Boston Post* (Boston, Massachusetts), March 8, 1894.

"A Sickening Spectacle." *Springfield Missouri Republican* (Springfield, Missouri), December 15, 1894.

"Stabbed to Death." *The Fitchburg Sentinel* (Fitchburg, Massachusetts), September 11, 1893.

"A Wife Murderer Convicted." *Carlisle Evening Herald* (Carlisle, Pennsylvania), March 9, 1894.

HOLDER ALONZO "LON" TRIPP

CRIME

Man kicked to death, suffering a fractured skull, on the railroad tracks east of The Narrows, in Fall River, Massachusetts, on July 10, 1897.

VICTIM

Holder Alonzo "Lon" Tripp, 52

ACCUSED

Jeremiah Manchester, 24

DETAILS

Holder Alonzo Tripp, a farmer in Westport, Massachusetts, was found dying on the New Bedford Road on July 10, 1897. According to *The New York Times*, Tripp died before a doctor could reach him. "Tripp lived on Fisher's Road, Westport, and until a week ago had as his housekeeper Sarah Readan [Reagan], who was also known as Sarah Smith. About a week ago, [Jeremiah] Manchester, who was infatuated with the woman, married her, and took her from Tripp's house to his own house, on Sanford's Road [sic]. The marriage and the removal of the woman caused much jealousy and bad feelings between the two men.

"Last night Manchester and his wife drove into Fall River, and Tripp also came to the city. The two men were drinking together in a saloon in Flint Village, and left the saloon in company. About 11:30 o'clock passengers on the last car on the New Bedford and Fall River Electric Line, when one mile out of the city, found Tripp in the road, his head on Mrs. Manchester's lap, with Mr. Manchester standing near by. Tripp's head was covered in blood, and he was fearfully bruised. He died within a half an hour.

"The passengers in the car detained Manchester until Fall River policemen placed him under arrest. He protested his innocence and told his story of the affair as follows:

"He said he started from Fall River for his home in Westport with his wife in their wagon. They stopped at the watering trough on Eastern Avenue, just on the outskirts of the city, to water their horse. While they were there Tripp drove by alone in his wagon. After their horse had finished drinking they followed. When they reached the point in the road where Tripp died their horses shied, but Manchester thought little about it and kept on the Sanford Road. There he overtook Tripp's team, but Tripp was not in sight. Manchester says he then associated the shying of the horse with the fact that Tripp was missing. Knowing that Tripp had been drinking and fearing that some accident had befallen him, he got into Tripp's wagon, turned the horses around, and telling his wife to follow, drove back to the place where he found Tripp lying in the middle of the road bruised and bleeding.

"An autopsy held this afternoon by Medical Examiner [William A.] Dolan and other physicians revealed the fact that death was caused by fractures of the skull. There were several fractures and many cuts and bruises, indicating that blows had been struck with some blunt instrument. It is believed by the police that the men met and quarreled about the woman and that Tripp was kicked to death. The woman in the course of her talk about the affair said: 'Both these men were crazy about me, but I had no hand in this.' There were blood stains on the prisoner's clothing and traces of blood were found in both wagons."

The Sun newspaper reported it differently. They stated that "for nearly ten years the woman lived as the common-law wife of Tripp. For four years she was frequently with Manchester, much against Tripp's wishes. As a result bitter feelings existed and when, then days ago, she married Manchester, Tripp vowed vengeance. ... A little beyond the city limits [Tripp] waited for Manchester, and when the latter drove along with his wife Tripp stopped them. He tried to induce the woman to go with him, and Manchester ordered him to go away. A fight in the road followed. Manchester, though smaller than Tripp, downed the latter and pounded him terribly, using a blunt instrument, probably a beer bottle. Tripp's skull was fractured in three places and his face was torn and discolored. The fatal wound was a deep split across the forehead."

According to the *Essex County Herald*, "The Manchesters have police records. A year ago the woman went to

Connecticut to live with a man named Bradshaw, but Tripp followed her and induced her to return."

THE TRIAL

Manchester was sentenced to eight years in prison.

OUTCOME

Jeremiah Manchester went insane while in prison and was transferred to the Taunton State Hospital.

AFTERWORD

Mrs. Jeremiah Manchester (Sarah Reagan) was arraigned in Fall River, Massachusetts, on July 20, 1897, on a charge of bigamy. Apparently, she was still married to William Reagan in Connecticut when she wed Mr. Manchester. This is important because if she can be proven guilty of bigamy, she can be compelled to testify against Manchester in his murder case.

Also of note is that Manchester's grandfather, Gideon, was murdered twenty years previously by James Clough, who was hanged for the crime.

FURTHER READING

"Alleged Bigamy." *The Courier-News* (Bridgewater, New Jersey), July 20, 1897.
"Brutal Murder Committed at Fall River." *Essex County Herald* (Guildhall, Vermont), July 16, 1897.
"Charged with Bigamy." *Daily Argosy* (Middletown, New York), July 20, 1987.
"Killed After a Fight." *The Sun* (New York, New York), July 12, 1897.
"Murder Near Fall River." *The New York Times*, July 12, 1897.
"Nothing in Annals of Fall River Attracted As Much Attention as Borden Murder Case," *Fall River Herald News* (Fall River, Massachusetts), September 19, 1958.

GALLERY

Jeremiah Manchester.
Fall River Daily Evening News.

LOUIS T. GORMLEY

CRIME

Accidental shooting by fellow Fall River Police Officer, August 23, 1898.

VICTIM

Louis T. Gormley, Fall River Police Officer, 30

ACCUSED

N/A

DETAILS

Badge # 55 was accidentally shot and killed by a fellow officer while they were pursuing a man on East Main Street wanted for neglecting his family. According to the Officer Down Memorial Page, "The suspect fell during the pursuit and as the officers tried to arrest him the second officer's firearm discharged and struck Officer Gormley." The *Fall River Herald News* further reports that "As the man ran south, the officers fired warning shots at him. Gormley ran around the block and got onto Lee Street, running west, just as the man turned to run east. Before Gormley could capture the man, one of the other officers fell and pistol fired. Gormley was shot and died."

THE TRIAL

There was no trial.

OUTCOME

It was determined that the gun of the other officer discharged by accident and a bullet struck and killed Gormley.

AFTERWORD

Gormley had served the department for six years and was only the second of four officers killed in the line of duty. He was a bachelor when he died and was buried in a private plot in St. Patrick's Cemetery. In 2012, remaining family members were presented with a flag and a posthumous medal of honor. A brass plaque were affixed to the foyer wall at the Fall River Police Department and a granite marker added to the memorial site that stands in front of the station.

FURTHER READING

"Louis T. Gormley." Officer Down Memorial Page. odmp.org.

O'Connor, Kevin. "FRPD will honor 2 heroic past officers who died doing duties." *Fall River Herald News*, April 15, 2012.

"Wednesday, August 24." *Burlington Weekly Free Press* (Burlington, Vermont), August 25, 1898.

CHAPTER 2
1900 TO 1929
TWO VIOLENT DECADES

In this book, there are mostly sad stories and endings, especially for the victims and their families. The events are also tragic for the accused and their families. But these events are true and intensely fascinating because they are real and occurred in areas that the reader may well know.

You may have walked the same streets where these dastardly deeds have been committed. After reading of these events, you may not again travel the streets of Fall River and New Bedford or the parks and trails the same carefree way. Drive along Seabury Street in Fall River and envision Harry O bleeding in the gutter or the police surrounding a body on Ferry Street. Even the suburbs of tranquil Somerset, Freetown, Fairhaven, Dartmouth, Westport, Little Compton, Tiverton, Swansea, Dighton, and Berkley take on a different demeanor. The serene images of seaweed on the beaches of Little Compton and the fun days at Baker's Beach or Davol Pond are now shattered by the memories of the dead lying along these shores.

It wasn't particularly difficult to discover the details of these murders, manslaughters, and mayhem on the SouthCoast because the crimes tended to appear on the front pages of local and regional newspapers. As is true even today, he dark side of humanity generates headline-grabbing coverage. Evil not only exists in faraway lands but on local street corners. While reading the following pages, you may find familiar names and the sad events of family, friends, neighbors, and neighborhoods.

The author did not understand, until very recently, why so many of these crimes remain open and unsolved. It was only through the advent of modern forensic science that these old cases can be solved. People still come forward with a clue or a DNA sample that turns the case around. In every one of these unsolved cases, families forever hold out hope for a solution to the mystery of a long departed loved one—sometimes with success. Most recently, the human remains of Steven DiSarro were found in a grave in Rhode Island after he went missing in 1993.

I will not tell you to enjoy this book. It is not a fun read. But it is a lasting tribute to those victims and their families who should never be forgotten.

IDA HOWARD

CRIME	Husband strangles wife to death in New Bedford, Massachusetts, on September 20, 1908
VICTIM	Ida Howard, 18
ACCUSED	William C. Howard, 24

DETAILS

William C. Howard, a private in the 52d Company of the United States Coast Artillery, stationed at Fort Rodman, New Bedford, had been arrested the year before for shooting and killing Edward Dewhurst, in Hazelwood Park, in New Bedford, Massachusetts. Dewhurst had been killed in 1905 but no one was charged for the murder. Howard's girlfriend, Grace F. Sturtevant, who was a witness to the shooting, kept the secret.

After his first 3-year enlistment expired, Howard went back to his home in Tennessee and married Ida there. He kept this information from Grace, even though he was still "paying much attention" to her. When Howard returned to New Bedford, he re-enlisted in the army and told Grace that Ida was his sister, Rhoda. In 1908, Ida revealed that Howard had killed Dewhurst and he was arrested and tried for the crime, facing the electric chair if found guilty. It was then that Grace Sturtevant came forward and told her story of being present at the death and that Howard had fired in self defense. Because of her testimony, Howard was acquitted.

It was only two months later that Howard's wife, Ida, died under mysterious circumstances.

THE TRIAL

At his trial for the murder of Ida Howard, testimony was presented that there was no trace of poison in Ida's stomach, that her body had several red-blue spots on the right side of her face, and that the night she disappeared, a woman's screams were heard near the bridge where her body was found the next day. Medical experts also testified that Ida had been choked to death and then thrown in the water; that she had not drowned.

Grace Sturtevant testified that after the Dewhurst manslaughter trial, Howard talked to her about divorcing Ida and marrying her. She said that they talked about this the night before Ida's death.

Howard was quite the Lothario, even recording in his "soldier's handbook" a list of "My Sweethearts" that included thirteen names. One of those on the list, Lena Watson, took the stand in Howard's defense and swore that she and Howard had spent from 8 p.m. until midnight on the night of the death of Ida at Fort Rodman in New Bedford. The prosecution's claim was that Howard had strangled his wife to death and threw her dead body in Appanagansett Bay at Padanaram, Dartmouth, Massachusetts, so that he would be free to marry another. William Howard's defense was that the death of Ida Howard was due to drowning and not strangulation or suffocation. He maintained throughout that his wife had committed suicide because she was despondent over her physical condition.

OUTCOME

William C. Howard was found guilty of murder in the second degree. He was sentenced to serve a life term in the state prison at Charlestown, Massachusetts.

AFTERWORD

To add yet another twist to the story of William C. Howard, soon after his conviction for the murder of Ida, Howard was identified as the man who fired the shot that killed Governor William Goebel of Kentucky, nine years previously.

The information could not be made public during his trial for killing Ida Howard as they would bias the jury and would have constituted "contempt of court."

According to the *Star Tribune*, "The police and detective forces of Kentucky have for years believed that Jim Howard, himself, did not kill Goebel, but that a young nephew [William] whom he brought down to the state capitol with him from the mountains, fired the shot from the office of Secretary of State Caleb Powers. This young man, under age at that time, fled to the mountains across the state line. It is known that he enlisted in the United States army. Governor Goebel was killed on January 10, 1900."

ADDENDUM

William Howard appears in federal census records for 1920, 1930, and 1940. He began serving his sentence at the Massachusetts State Prison in Charlestown, where he was a nurse working in the prison hospital. In 1930 he is reported to be married, but there are no records of this wedding or the name of his new wife. In 1940 William is listed as an inmate of the Lawrence Hospital (prison system) and now 55 years old. No further information has been obtained.

FURTHER READING

"Accused of Three-Year-Old Murder." *New-York Tribune* (New York, New York), July 21, 1908.

"Charged with Murder." *Altoona Tribune* (Altoona, Pennsylvania), September 25, 1908.

"Grace Sturtevant Gives Testimony." *The Portsmouth Herald* (Portsmouth, New Hampshire), Marcy 2, 1909.

"Like Billy Brown Case." *The Baltimore Sun* (Baltimore, Maryland), March 8, 1909.

"Life Sentence for Wife Slayer." *Pittsburgh Post-Gazette* (Pittsburgh, Pennsylvania), March 11, 1909.

"Murder Demonstration in Court." *New-York Tribune* (New York, New York), February 27, 1909.

"No Trace of Poison Found in Stomach." *The Atlanta Constitution* (Atlanta, Georgia), February 28, 1909.

"Oaths for a Soldier." *Washington Post* (Washington, District of Columbia), March 7, 1909.

"Posed as Single Man." *Fitchburg Sentinel* (Fitchburg, Massachusetts), Marcy 2, 1909.

"Private Howard Arrested." *Fitchburg Sentinel* (Fitchburg, Massachusetts), September 23, 1908.

"Real Slayer of Goebel is Found." *Star Tribune* (Minneapolis, Minnesota), March 15, 1909.

"Suicide Claim by Howard Defense." *The Portsmouth Herald* (Portsmouth, New Hampshire), March 9, 1909.

"Trial Nearing End." *Fitchburg Sentinel* (Fitchburg, Massachusetts), March 9, 1909.

AMELIA ST. JEAN

CRIME

Dismemberment at death as the result of a botched abortion, October 8, 1909. Body parts discovered in Tiverton, Rhode Island, and Fall River, Massachusetts. Death occurred in Fall River.

VICTIM

Amelia St. Jean, 19

ACCUSED

Dr. "Professor" Frank B. Hill, 44

DETAILS

Following a positive identification of the dismembered body of Amelia St. Jean, whose remains were discovered by a postal worker strewn along Bulgarmarsh Road, in Tiverton, Rhode Island, Wilfred Thibault, 26, chauffeur for Attorney William E. Fuller, Jr., and Professor Frank Hill, 44, herb doctor, were initially charged with causing her death. Both men denied taking part in the murder. Hill was implicated because his name was found on a portion of the case in which part of St. Jean's torso was discovered.

Thibault was described in the *Allentown Democrat* as "a little, stoop shouldered man about twenty-six years old. He is not the sort of man whose appearance would attract a woman. He looks weak, almost consumptive." The same paper described Hill as "a stockily built, mustached person, with a swaggering, confident manner." They described Miss St. Jean as having a "venturesome career for a girl of nineteen and a mill worker. She was far above the ordinary mill workers in intelligence and had been called the prettiest working girl in Woonsocket. ... She had been with the 'Human Fish' company, which exhibited at fairs in Maine and elsewhere during the summer, having returned about six weeks ago."

Tiverton Medical Examiner Dr. Edward P. Stimson examined the remains. According to *Parallel Lives*, St.

Jean was "described as 'plump [and] well-nourished, [the torso] measured only twenty-three inches in length,' indicating that, in life, the young woman had been 'about 4 feet, 10 inches in height, certainly not more than five feet.' Outside of a few 'smooches of blood and, here and there, a little dirt' there were no other marks upon the flesh. Further investigation by the medical examiner determined that the 'unknown girl was pregnant. The appearances [were] that an abortion had been attempted.'"

According to a report in *The Sun*, the story of the crime is as follows: Hill said he had refused to perform a "criminal operation" (i.e. abortion) that St. Jean had requested, but she "appeared in his herb store and attempted the operation herself. ... Hill thought she was dead. He went into a frenzy of fear and the first and only thing he thought of was to get rid of her body rather than have it discovered in his shop. He seized a knife and saw that were near at hand and severed the right leg. Then he cut up the rest of the body. ... The work of dismembering took about two hours. That same night he hired a carriage and took the torso and limbs into the neighboring town of Tiverton and got rid of them. The next Saturday night he took the head in a basket to a cemetery in this city and threw it in a hole there."

The dismembered left leg and right thigh was discovered on Monday, October 17, and the torso found Tuesday about 500 yards away from the other parts. Wednesday, October 19, the right leg and two arms were found in another spot. Search for the head continued until Hill reported its whereabouts in his confession.

Dr Stimson believed that St. Jean had received an abortion, but that it was not successful and not the cause of her death. According to *Parallel Lives*, Stimson "had previously determined that the cause of death could have been 'anemia, probably caused by the fact that the murderer had cut his victim's throat and then begun dismembering the body while the girl was still alive.'" Other physicians, however, could not find evidence of an abortion but added that "'such evidence might have been destroyed by the Stimson autopsy.'"

Hill pleaded not guilty to the crime and while in prison awaiting trial wrote his wife and daughter that he was as "innocent as the babe unborn of this crime." Following the Grand Jury, an indictment was issued for manslaughter.

| THE TRIAL | By the time of the trial, which began in the second week of November, Hill had changed to his plea to guilty. According to *The Washington Post*, "Hill's attorney told the court that the St. Jean girl had visited Hill by appointment, and while there had performed an operation upon herself." |

According to *Parallel Lives*, in his own words, Hill said:

> I first got water and threw it in her face ... on using water I rubbed her wrists. Her eyes were almost closed then. I do not know if they finally closed themselves. After getting water I noticed her lips were turning black; her finger nails were blue. I did not try pulse or heart beat, but did try glass over her mouth. Am sure there was no grasp, or choking or foaming at the mouth ... I then used ammonia, which I had in [a] pint bottle in the closet. It was clear ammonia. I held that under her nostrils two or three times. It had no effect on her. I worked over her three hours off and on. Her face kept darkening all the time.
>
> ...
>
> I first cut off the right leg, cutting the flesh to the bone, and then using the saw. No blood spurted at the first cut of the knife. The eyes were not closed then. I had shut them but they would not stay closed. Next cut off the head and then found the instrument in her skirts or on the floor, where it had fallen from her skirts. The clothes were taken off in the closet. No blood was noticed on the instrument, which was disposed by throwing it down the toilet. Did so to get rid of it.

Quickly disposing of the body parts, Hill admits to keeping the head in his shop for a few days, and conducted business as usual while it was in the water closet (bathroom). According to *Parallel Lives*, "'As near as he could describe the place, he disposed of the head on the west side of Robeson street, a few feet from the street railway switch there, and not far from St. Patrick's cemetery.' It was wrapped in a black petticoat."

OUTCOME

The court accepted Hill's plea of guilty of manslaughter. Frank Hill, the skin specialist, was sentenced to seven to ten years of hard labor.

FURTHER READING

"Body Identified." *The Morning News* (Wilmington, Delaware), October 15, 1909.

"Body was in Suitcase." *Fall River Evening News*, October 11, 1909.

"Doctor and Chauffeur Arrested in St. Jean Case at Fall River." *Detroit Free Press* (Detroit, Michigan), October 15, 1909.

"Girl's Death Cleared Up." *The Sun* (New York, New York), November 10, 1909.

"Girl's Missing Head Found." *The Washington Post* (Washington, D.C.), November 10, 1909.

"Held as Suspects." *The Courier-News* (Bridgewater, New Jersey), October 15, 1909.

"'Herb Doctor' and Chauffeur." *Fitchburg Daily Sentinel* (Fitchburg, Massachusetts), October 15, 1909.

"Herb Doctor Pleads Guilty." *Stevens Point Daily Journal* (Stevens Point, Wisconsin), November 10, 1909.

"Herb Doctor Sentenced." *Mount Carmel Item* (Mount Carmel, Pennsylvania), November 18, 1909.

Martins, Michael and Dennis Binette. *Parallel Lives: A Social History of Lizzie A. Borden and Her Fall River*. Fall River Historical Society, 2010.

"Nothing in Annals of Fall River Attracted As Much Attention as Borden Murder Case," *Fall River Herald News* (Fall River, Massachusetts), September 19, 1958.

"St. Jean Mystery." *The Portsmouth Daily Herald* (Portsmouth, New Hampshire), October 21, 1909.

"Suitcase Victim's Head Found." *The Baltimore Sun* (Baltimore, Maryland), November 10, 1909.

"Suspects Deny Murdering Girl. *The Allentown Democrat* (Allentown, Pennsylvania), October 16, 1909.

"Thibault Let Go But Will Witness." *Altoona Tribune* (Altoona, Pennsylvania), October 23, 1909.

"Thinks Girl Dead, Dismembers Her." *Detroit Free Press* (Detroit, Michigan), November 10, 1909.

"Two Held for Girl's Death." *The Courier-News* (Bridgewater, New Jersey), October 16, 1909.

"Two Men Now in Prison in Tiverton Mystery." *The Brooklyn Daily Eagle* (Brooklyn, New York), October 15, 1909.

"Two Suspects are Detained." *Portsmouth Daily Herald* (Portsmouth, New Hampshire), October 15, 1909.

GALLERY

Amelia St. Jean. *The Courier-News*, October 16, 1909.

ALMEDA ALBERTINE "TINA" HALL FANNING

CRIME

Husband kills wife with a hatchet in Westport, Mass-achusetts, and then drives to the police station in New Bedford, Massachusetts, presents a confession letter, and commits suicide with a gun in front of the police, on July 25, 1909.

VICTIM

Almeda Albertine "Tina" Hall Fanning, 27

ACCUSED

Robert M. Fanning, 26

DETAILS

Using an old tomahawk which he supposedly dug up from a grave of a dead Indian chief in Westport, Robert M. Fanning hacked his wife, known as Tina, to death on the west side of Lyon's Brook, then hid her body in the bushes. Fanning then returned to his home in Westport, Massachusetts, wrote a letter (see below) addressed to the chief of police in New Bedford, drove to the police, confessed to the crime, presented the letter, and shot himself in the head with a gun in front of the startled officers.

According to the *Philadelphia Inquirer*, "Fanning arrived at the police station here about 2 o'clock this morning in his automobile. He was in such a condition that it was with difficulty he could make himself understood. He produced a letter from his pocket and after making several futile attempt to read it himself handed it to Lieutenant Comstock, the man in charge.

"As the lieutenant read the letter he asked: 'What do you want me to do about it?'

"'Just this,' was the reply, and Fanning with a quick motion produced a big revolver, placed the muzzle to his mouth and fired. He fell dead instantly.

"The couple had a violent quarrel yesterday and Mrs. Fanning told her husband that she would no longer live with him. The couple went for a walk to talk over the matter and Mrs. Fanning did not return."

Because of its unusual and gory nature, this case received nationwide coverage in major newspapers, including *The New York Times*, the *Washington Post*, the *Baltimore Sun*, and the *Philadelphia Inquirer*.

Fanning's Letter: "To Woman It May Concern: I am very, very sorry for what has occurred, and the police can judge for themselves if I was not too hasty and likewise my wife. God bless her. My baby is still living by this time. God bless her, and I hope she will never know what happened to her dead father and mother. I loved my child better than myself. May God give me his blessings and to my child everlasting good will. I have had a good deal to put up with, and the end is near.

"Trusting my baby will have the best of care, as she is one of the best babies that ever lived. It is hard to leave such a happy child, but my God, I must.

"Oh, God, I wish I could live to comfort my child; she has everything to live for. I hope she will benefit by it, as there is enough for her to be wealthy. I would like to have my baby join us but as cruel as I am, I have no heart for such. My wife's body lays on the west side of Lyon's Brook, about 50 feet to the south of the bushes. Please give it your immediate attention and remove same as soon as possible. At my request please bury us both together. Trusting you will do your duty, I remain, Yours very truly, Robert M. Fanning

"P.S. Don't fail to look for my wife's body and remove same as soon as possible. Oh, my God, what have I done * * * for baby?

"P.S. Be sure and put my baby in good hands. My folks will take her, as I wish, which is my last wish. Hoping my baby will be looked after, as I know my folks will attend to it, good-by, pa and ma, brothers and sisters and to all my friends. God bless you all, and not forgetting my own flesh and blood, my baby. Mrs. Murray is a kind woman, and I must not forget her; God bless her. I am sorry for what I have done. Please give my ring and belongings to my brother Will."

Tina was the daughter of George Hall, who was said to have been one of the wealthiest men in Westport at one time, with an income of $15,000 a year. Tina had reportedly been married three times, her first marriage occurring when she was sixteen years old. Fanning's parents were of modest means and lived in Providence, Rhode Island.

Fanning frequently quarreled with George Hall over the running of Hall's estate, as Fanning was said to have been manager at one time while Hall was in a sanitarium. The housekeeper, Mrs. Murray, reported that Fanning has recently been drinking quite heavily and fighting with his wife.

According to *The New York Times*, Tina "was regarded as one of the prettiest girls in Westport and a great favorite. She was ... of medium height, and a striking brunette. For a year or two the young couple were very happy. Fanning lived the life of a country gentleman, sported diamond rings, rode about in automobiles, and apparently adored his wife.

"After a time he began to drink, and, according to the Westport gossip, liquor was the cause of the tragedy. Mrs. Fanning left the house at 8 o'clock and never returned. She had declared that because of his drunkenness and cruelty she would never live with him again. The couple went for a walk to talk the matter over and that was the last seen of the woman until her body was found."

THE TRIAL

Because this was essentially a murder/suicide, there was no trial, just intense speculation as to the cause of the crime.

FURTHER READING

"He Tomahawks His Young Wife." *The Marion Weekly Star* (Marion, Ohio), July 31, 1909.

"Killed Wife and Himself." *The Evening Journal* (Wilmington, Delaware), July 26, 1909.

"Killed Wife and Self." *The Brooklyn Eagle* (Brooklyn, New York), July 26, 1909.

"Slays Wealthy Wife Then Kills Himself." *The New York Times* (New York, New York), July 27, 1909.

"Told Police of Murder." *Fitchburg Sentinel* (Fitchburg, Massachusetts), July 26, 1909.

"Tomahawks Wife, Motors to Police and Kills Himself." *The Philadelphia Inquirer* (Philadelphia, Pennsylvania), July 27, 1909.

SARAH CROPPER

CRIME

Back yard altercation in Fall River, Massachusetts, on September 23, 1909, between mother and son, resulting in death.

VICTIM

Sarah Cropper, a widow, 59

ACCUSED

Peter Cropper, 36, son

DETAILS

Peter Cropper and his sister were engaged in an altercation in their yard at 922 South Main Street in Fall River when their mother, Sarah, intervened. Peter turned his anger on his mother, throwing a chair and then a stick at her prior to hitting her in the back with an iron ash can that knocked her to the ground. She died of her injuries the following day in the hospital.

THE TRIAL

Peter Cropper was charged with assault and battery, which was upgraded to manslaughter when she died a few days later.

OUTCOME

Peter Cropper served six months in the prison for this crime.

MORRIS SCHWARTZ

CRIME	Murder in a pool hall on Seventh Street, in Fall River, Massachusetts, on June 3, 1911, with razor and hammer.
VICTIM	Morris Schwartz, 28
ACCUSED	Edmund Berube, 34

DETAILS

Edmund Berube, a French-Canadian spinner at Stafford Mill, used a hammer and a razor to kill Schwartz. According to the *Fall River Herald News*, "Police said that Berube used the hammer first, hitting the victim on the back of the head. While unconscious on the floor of his Seventh street pool room, Schwartz' throat was slashed by a razor blade. The victim died en route to the Union Hospital.

"Accounts of the event say that Berube calmly walked into Central Police Station and gave himself up. Before his trial he laughed and sang in his cell. His actions were described as 'strange.' He insisted on posting for a *Herald* photographer."

THE TRIAL

The grand jury heard a plea of insanity from Berube who had previously spent time in the Taunton State Hospital. He was indicted on a charge of murder in the first degree.

OUTCOME

Berube was found guilty and sentenced to life in prison in solitary confinement in Charleston, Massachusetts.

AFTERWORD

After serving twenty-one years of his sentence, Berube sent a letter to his lawyer stating how happy he was in jail and blaming "booze and poker" for his downfall. The 1920, 1930, and 1940 federal census list an Edmund Berube as living in the State Hospital for the Criminally Insane in Bridgewater, Massachusetts.

FURTHER READING

"Nothing in Annals of Fall River Attracted As Much Attention as Borden Murder Case," *Fall River Herald News* (Fall River, Massachusetts), September 19, 1958.

MRS. DELIA PHANEUF

CRIME

Husband shot and killed his wife at home on January 2, 1912, in Fall River, Massachusetts.

VICTIM

Delia Phaneuf, wife, 24

ACCUSED

Arthur Phaneuf, 36, husband

DETAILS

After working at a logging camp in the Maine woods, Arthur Phaneuf returned to Fall River vowing to kill his young wife at the home of her mother on Harrison Street in the Flint section of the city. And he did.

THE TRIAL

Phaneuf was indicted for first-degree murder by the grand jury.

OUTCOME

Records are missing.

GALLERY

Arthur Phaneuf. *Fall River Daily Globe.*

DOMBA PEREMEBIDA

CRIME

A domestic (maid) was slashed to death with a razor on March 14, 1914, on Eagan's Court, off Spring Street, in the downtown area of Fall River, Massachusetts.

VICTIM

Mrs. Domba Peremebida, aka Diana Bialaska, 27 (Because of the unusual nature of her name, it is spelled differently in every account of this case: Domba Perembida, Donka Peremebida, Donba Poremebida.)

ACCUSED

Antone "Tony" Retkovitz, 30

DETAILS

Domba Peremebida was employed by Jacob Maker of 182 Spring Street as a domestic. She was found with her throat slashed from ear to ear by means of a razor in the rear of the Spring Street home.

THE TRIAL

The jury in Fall River Superior Court, after a brief trial, returned a verdict of guilty in the first degree. Retkovitz was granted a second trial. His attorney negotiated a verdict of second-degree murder with a life sentence. Retkovitz objected to the arrangement that his attorney, Frank M. Silvia, had procured for him and the trial was held much to the chagrin of the defendant.

OUTCOME

A second trial was held due to the good lawyering of Atty. Silvia but the outcome was the same—guilty in the first degree.

AFTERWORD

Antone "Tony" Retkovitz was electrocuted in the state prison on March 13, 1916. The current was applied at 12:05 and Retkovitz was officially pronounced dead at 12:15. He protested his innocence to the end.

FURTHER READING

"Boston, Massachusetts." *The Wilmington Morning Star* (Wilmington, North Carolina), March 14, 1916.

"Fall River Murderer Executed." *Hartford Courant* (Hartford, Connecticut), March 14, 1916.

"Nothing in Annals of Fall River Attracted As Much Attention as Borden Murder Case," *Fall River Herald News* (Fall River, Massachusetts), September 19, 1958.

"Retkovitz' Trial is Begun." *Fitchburg Sentinel* (Fitchburg, Massachusetts), January 26, 1916.

JESSE WATT

CRIME	Shooting and stabbing on a train by a circus employee on June 13, 1914, in Fall River, Massachusetts.
VICTIM	Jesse Watt, 30
ACCUSED	Alonzo Bell, 29, alias Brown
DETAILS	Watt and Bell, two circus employees from Barnum and Bailey, were shooting dice in a sleeper car on a train in the yard at the Watuppa Station in Fall River, when a shouting match erupted and Jesse Watt was stabbed innumerable times and fatally shot. Bell panicked and jumped another train to New York City where he held out for months before being found hiding in a boarding house by Manhattan detectives and sent back to Fall River to face charges.
THE TRIAL	Bell did not contest any of the charges and was immediately convicted within seven minutes and sent to prison. Watts had previously assaulted Bell but that was never brought up at the trial.
OUTCOME	In December of 1914, Bell was found guilty of murder in the second degree and ordered to spend the rest of his life in State Prison at Charlestown, Massachusetts.
FURTHER READING	"Life Sentence for Slayer." *Fitchburg Sentinel* (Fitchburg, Massachusetts), December 3, 1914. "Nothing in Annals of Fall River Attracted As Much Attention as Borden Murder Case," *Fall River Herald News* (Fall River, Massachusetts), September 19, 1958.
GALLERY	 Alonzo Bell. *Fall River Daily Globe.*

SAM HADFIELD

CRIME	Deputy Sheriff was shot in the home of the accused at 692 Second Street in Fall River, Massachusetts, on May 15, 1915.
VICTIM	Deputy Sheriff Sam Hadfield, 60
ACCUSED	Catharine Marcella McCloskey, 45
DETAILS	Deputy Sheriff Sam Hadfield and two assistants attempted to enter the Catharine McCloskey's home to serve her legal papers on the order of the court. According to the *Boston Post*, "Hadfield entered the house though a window after being refused admission ... [a warrent to send] the five woman to the insane hospital was issued a day or two ago. Deputy Sheriff Hadfield removed two of the women to the hospital yesterday, and went back to the house this afternoon to serve ..." Apparently the five women, Catharine and her four maiden sisters, were adjudged insane and were in the process of being removed to the state asylum in Taunton, Massachusetts. Catharine thought that Hadfield was coming after her to do violence so she shot him in the neck, which resulted in his instant death.
THE TRIAL	Catherine McCloskey was found insane and committed to Taunton State Hospital.
AFTERWORD	Hadfield was born in 1855 in Durkinfield, Greater Manchester, England. He was survived by three children.
FURTHER READING	"Deputy Murdered While Arresting 3 Crazy Sisters." *Pittsburgh Daily Post* (Pittsburgh, Pennsylvania), May 14, 1915. "Is Killed by a Woman." *Boston Post*, May 14, 1915. "Killed by Insane Woman." *Boston Evening Globe*, May 13, 1915.

"Nothing in Annals of Fall River Attracted As Much Attention
as Borden Murder Case," *Fall River Herald News* (Fall River,
Massachusetts), September 19, 1958.

GALLERY

Left: Catharine McCloskey. *Right:* Sam Hadfield. *Fall River Daily Globe.*

WILLIAM A. BENNETT

CRIME

Man from Lynn, Massachusetts, was struck from behind and killed while visiting Fairhaven, Massachusetts, on October 14, 1916.

VICTIM

William A. Bennett, 56

ACCUSED

Unknown

DETAILS

William A. Bennett was visiting her daughter, Helen, Mrs. Warren Gould, who had three months previously given birth to a son, when he was struck from behind on Friday, October 13, 1916, with a heavy instrument as he was standing in front of the waiting station near the Fairhaven Bridge. He never regained consciousness and died from his injuries the next day.

"A teamster, who witnessed the attack, told police that he saw a slender man walk deliberately up to Bennett, strike him and then run away. No motive for the assault is known. Bennett's family say he had no enemies so far as they knew and that, outside of his own small circle of relatives here, he was a stranger to the community. The police were unable to find any clue today, and they are inclined to the theory that Bennett was mistaken for some one else" (*Hartford Courant*).

OUTCOME

There were no arrests so there was no trial. Unsolved.

FURTHER READING

"Police Investigate Mysterious Murder." *Hartford Courant* (Hartford, Connecticut) October 16, 1916.
"Visitor Slain by Stranger." *Boston Post* (Boston, Massachusetts), October 16, 1916.
"Waylayed and Blackjacked." *Fitchburg Sentinel* (Fitchburg, Massachusetts), October 14, 1916.

ANNIE DONOVAN BROWN

CRIME	Husband strangled, stabbed, and cut his young bride into pieces in Fall River, Massachusetts, approximately July 4, 1918.
VICTIM	Annie Donovan Brown, 20
ACCUSED	William T. "Tattoo" Brown, 42
DETAILS	According to the *Boston Post*, "about a month ago [June, 1918] Annie Donovan and a man known as Brown appeared at the lodging house in 110 Cedar Street [Fall River] and secured a room. The girl was widely known about the city. Born here, the daughter of a poor family—her father is Patrick Donovan, a coal passer on ships—she had gained much notoriety, partly because of the misdoings of her brothers, 'Red' Donovan, now serving a sentence in the State prison at Charlestown [Massachusetts], and partly because of her own misdoings. She had been frequently brought before the police, once for the sale of liquor to sailors. Up to the time of taking the rooms in the Cedar street house, however, the girl had not been about the city for some time. During part of her absence she had been with a sister in Waterbury, Conn., it is understood. The rest of the time she had just been 'away.'

"When she first returned she called on a member of her family, accompanied by the man known as Brown. He was her husband, she said, and he produced a marriage license. The relative did not see her again, but heard of her going to the Cedar street house. To that house the police traced her. She was remembered at once by those in the house, but none had seen her since about the Fourth of July. Where she had gone none could tell. She had just disappeared."

Brown, a draftsman and tattoo artist, throttled his young bride, dismembered her, and put her body parts into sacks and threw them into the Mount Hope Bay and the Taunton River. "Tattoo" left town, moved to Tennessee, and was discovered in 1932 when he applied for a veteran pension for the time he served in the Spanish-American War. Authorities searched for years for the name of the victim and at one point, due to her size, referenced her as Miss "Cornfed."

THE TRIAL

After being on the run for years, Brown was found guilty.

OUTCOME

He was sentenced to life and one day in prison.

FURTHER READING

"Believe Victim is Identified." *Boston Post* (Boston, Massachusetts), July 29, 1918.
"Man Held for Murder." *Fitchburg Sentinel* (Fitchburg, Massachusetts), August 17, 1918.

GALLERY

Left: William T. "Tattoo" Brown. *Right:* Annie Donovan Brown.
Images courtesy of the Fall River Herald News.

MANUEL C. ALMEIDA, JR.

CRIME

The victim was shot and killed with an automatic revolver in Somerset, Massachusetts, on January 9, 1918.

VICTIM

Manuel Almeida, Jr., 25

ACCUSED

Philip W. Thorpe, 26

DETAILS

Manuel Almeida, Jr., was a well-liked, with no known enemies, jitney driver for a taxi company that ran between Fall River and New Bedford, Massachusetts. Almeida was removed from the jitney, thrown over a stone wall, and left in a field to die. According to *The Brooklyn Daily Eagle* (January 19, 1918), Almeida "had been shot through the head and there were four bullet holes in his right shoulder." The event was thought to be caused by a jealous Philip W. Thorpe. Almeida was having an affair with Thorpe's ex-wife and helped her gain a divorce from her husband. Almeida had two diamond rings on his person from Mrs. Thorpe when he was killed.

According to *The Brooklyn Daily Eagle* (January 20, 1918), police officials requested the Huntington, Long Island, police to detain Philip Thorpe, a chauffeur, "in connection with the murder of Manuel C. Almeida, on January 9, because they wished to question him about a revolver which they believe may have been the weapon used by Almeida's slayer. The revolver was purchased in Providence, R.I., two days before the murder and was pawned later by a man giving the name of Frank Thomas."

Thorpe was apprehended in Huntington, Long Island, on January 12, and extradited to Fall River.

THE TRIAL

Thorpe pleaded guilty to second-degree murder.

OUTCOME

He was sentenced to life and one day in prison.

AFTERWORD

According to the *Hartford Courant* (June 8, 1934), Thorpe had been playing the violin on the radio during his stay in prison, which "brought hundreds of letters requesting his release and even stirred the interest of Henry Ford in the case ... Today before the State Board of Pardons and parole, he told once more the story of self-defense related at his trial; how an argument had arisen over the fare to Providence, R.I.; how he thought he saw Almeida reach for a gun, although it was afterward developed the driver was unarmed, and how he shot him down.

"To Thorpe's plea for liberty, Almeida's brother, Joseph, also of Fall River, entered in a tense scene at the prison, a vigorous protest. 'My brother was a good boy,' he cried. 'He worked hard. He saved money. He bought his own cab. Then this happened and my mother,' his voice broke, 'she died of a broken heart.'

"State Senator L. Theo Woolfenden of New Bedford represented Thorpe, and his father, John Thorpe, testified to his previous good character as did a half-sister, Ruth Crapo of Fall River. In recent years Thorpe has had charge of all prison musical activities. It was in 1925 that Ford, passing through Boston, related having heard Thorpe play, and asked concerning his case."

Thorpe was pardoned for his crime by Governor James M. Curley in 1936.

FURTHER READING

"Gets Life Sentence for Murder." *Hartford Courant* (Hartford, Connecticut), February 20, 1918.

"Mass. Lifer, Violin Artist, Asks Pardon." *Hartford Courant* (Hartford, Connecticut), June 8, 1934.

"Nothing in Annals of Fall River Attracted As Much Attention as Borden Murder Case," *Fall River Herald News* (Fall River, Massachusetts), September 19, 1958.

"Special to The Eagle." *The Brooklyn Daily Eagle* (Brooklyn, New York), January 19, 1918.

"To Extradite Thorpe." *The Brooklyn Daily Eagle* (Brooklyn, New York), January 20, 1918.

GALLERY

ALMEIDA HAD TWO ROLLS AND DIAMONDS

"This photograph taken in the Central Police station garage where the Almeida murder car is now stored. The rope which appears in the photograph was affixed to the auto after it was recovered to prevent persons without authority from tampering with the machine. The blood-soaked cushion on which Almeida sat is shown on the radiator." *Fall River Evening Herald.*

MARY AND JENNIE DEMSKEY

CRIME	Double axe murder at home at 74 Hunter Street, in Fall River, Massachusetts, by husband/step-father, on August 15, 1922.
VICTIMS	Mary Demskey, wife, 31, and step–daughter, Jennie, 18
ACCUSED	Peter Demskey, 34
DETAILS	Peter Demskey, laborer (teemer), and wife Mary had been having disputes over the his lack of employment. He axed to death both his wife and step-daughter at home. According to *The Bridgeport Telegram*, Demskey "informed the police that he had clubbed his wife, Mary, and 14-year-old [sic] step-daughter, over the head with an axe following a quarrel."
THE TRIAL	Demskey was declared insane after the event, and was committed to Bridgewater State Hospital. Demskey died in the hospital during the year he was committed.
AFTERWORD	The Demskey's had a total of six children. The surviving children include: William, age 8, Agatha, age 7, Rosie, age 6, Dorothy, age 5, and Paul, age 3. Both Peter and Mary were born in Poland.
FURTHER READING	"Man Held in Murder of Wife and Daughter." *The Caledonian-Record* (St. Johnsbury, Vermont), August 23, 1922. "Nothing in Annals of Fall River Attracted As Much Attention as Borden Murder Case," *Fall River Herald News* (Fall River, Massachusetts), September 19, 1958. "Used Axe to Kill Wife and Step Daughter." *The Bridgeport Telegram* (Bridgeport, Connecticut), August 17, 1922.

JOSEPH LAFLAMME AND JAMES CLARKE

CRIME

Multiple deaths by shooting on Stafford Road, in Fall River, Massachusetts, on August 12, 1923.

VICTIMS

Joseph LaFlamme and James Clarke, 32 and 61

ACCUSED

John Edward Kennedy, 27

DETAILS

Joseph LaFlamme, carpenter, and James Clarke, tea salesman, were in the proverbial wrong place at the wrong time when John Edward Kennedy walked into the yard at Clarke's house where Clarke was chatting with Kennedy's father in the Stafford Road section of the Fall River and opened fire. According to the *Poughkeepsie Eagle-News*, young Kennedy was heard to say, "Here are three pills for each of you." Then he "drew a revolver and fired one shot, killing Clarke instantly. LaFlamme, a neighbor, heard the shooting and came into the yard. At once, according to witnesses, Kennedy drew his revolver again, held it close to LaFlamme's face, and fired."

Kennedy was captured by Mounted Police Officer Daniel F. Sullivan after a street fight, during which Kennedy was shot twice. Sullivan was later hailed a hero for his efforts and presented with a watch by residents of the Stafford Road area.

According to a report in the *Fitchburg Sentinel*, "the police are inclined to believe that troubles with his family unbalanced Kennedy's mind and led to this killing. The father of the boy is sure the son meant to kill him first, but turned the gun on Clarke instead."

Kennedy, who resided in a shack in the woods near the South Watuppa Pond, had once attempted suicide by drowning off Stone Bridge in Tiverton, Rhode Island.

THE TRIAL

Kennedy was declared insane on February 19, 1924.

AFTERWORD

On April 23, 1936, Kennedy hanged himself with his suspenders in the bathroom at Bridgewater State Hospital.

FURTHER READING

"Boy Who Killed Two Believed Insane." *Fitchburg Sentinel* (Fitchburg, Massachusetts), August 13, 1923.

"Kills Two: Third May Die." *Harrisburg Telegraph* (Harrisburg, Pennsylvania), August 13, 1923.

"Man Runs Wild: Two Are Killed." *Poughkeepsie Eagle-News* (Poughkeepsie, New York), August 13, 1923.

"Nothing in Annals of Fall River Attracted As Much Attention as Borden Murder Case," *Fall River Herald News* (Fall River, Massachusetts), September 19, 1958.

"Runs Amuck and Kills Two." *The Wilkes-Barre Record* (Wilkes-Barre, Pennsylvania), August 13, 1923.

"Two Killed and Third Wounded by Gunman." *The Philadelphia Inquirer* (Philadelphia, Pennsylvania), August 13, 1923.

GALLERY

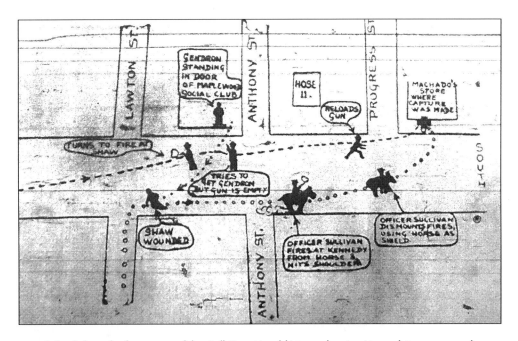

Partial sketch from the front page of the *Fall River Herald News,* showing Kennedy's capture at the corner of Progress Street and Stafford Road, the gun battle, and where Kennedy was wounded.

James M. Clarke. *Image courtesy of the Fall River Herald News.*

Police Officer Daniel Sullivan. *Image courtesy of the Fall River Herald News.*

BERNARD ROSENFELD

CRIME

Murder by an iron to the head at 210 South Main Street, in Fall River, Massachusetts, on October 2, 1924.

VICTIM

Bernard Rosenfeld, 17

ACCUSED

Frederick Bengton, 35

DETAILS

Teenager Bernard Rosenfeld was working at his father's (Benjamin Rosenfeld) store, Star Tailoring & Cleaning, at 210 South Main Street, when an argument ensued between Bengton and young Rosenfeld about keeping the door to the establishment opened or closed. Bengton became enraged and hit the young man in the head with a flat iron and killed him.

THE TRIAL

Frederick Bengton was convicted.

OUTCOME

Bengton was sent to Bridgewater State Hospital for the criminally insane on November 19, 1924.

FURTHER READING

"Nothing in Annals of Fall River Attracted As Much Attention as Borden Murder Case," *Fall River Herald News* (Fall River, Massachusetts), September 19, 1958.

MARIE LAPOINTE

CRIME
Husband beats wife to death in Greenwood Park, Westport, Massachusetts, on June 2, 1925.

VICTIM
Marie LaPointe, wife, 45

ACCUSED
Elle LaPointe, husband, 45

DETAILS
Elle LaPointe was a mason and reportedly a good worker when sober. On June 2, 1925, he was drinking heavily and went into a rage, beating his wife to death in their home in Westport. She was found naked and mutilated in the rear yard by a 75-year-old-veteran of the Civil War. The LaPointes had a nine-year-old daughter.

THE TRIAL
Elle LaPointe was allowed to plead guilty to manslaughter after being charged with beating Marie in an intoxicated rampage.

OUTCOME
LaPointe was sentenced to fifteen to twenty years in solitary confinement in prison.

FURTHER READING
"Find Woman's Body." *Times Herald* (Olean, New York), June 3, 1925.
"Nothing in Annals of Fall River Attracted As Much Attention as Borden Murder Case," *Fall River Herald News* (Fall River, Massachusetts), September 19, 1958.

DONALDA STEFANSKI

CRIME

Murder/suicide at 200 Broadway, Fall River, Massachusetts, on June 8, 1925.

VICTIM

Donalda Stefanski, wife, 31

ACCUSED

Frank Stefanski, husband, 31

DETAILS

Frank and Donalda Stefanski had been married for only two years and separated for four months when the murder/suicide took place on Broadway in Fall River. Frank shot Donalda five times and himself once. Jealousy was thought to be the motive. Donalda was described as a crippled dressmaker.

OUTCOME

Accused committed suicide before he could be arrested or charged.

FURTHER READING

"Nothing in Annals of Fall River Attracted As Much Attention as Borden Murder Case," *Fall River Herald News* (Fall River, Massachusetts), September 19, 1958.

LOUIS CHOUINARD

CRIME

Murder committed during the course of the robbery at 31 Choate Street in Fall River, Massachusetts, on December 5, 1925.

VICTIM

Louis Chouinard, 63

ACCUSED

Unknown

DETAILS

According to the *Hartford Courant*, Louis Chouinard was fatally wounded in the abdomen "in an unsuccessful attempt to rob him of $1,000 in store receipts which he was bringing home last night. ... He was shot down as he alighted from his automobile. His son and partner, Auguste, who was in the car, escaped death only because the revolver which the bandit placed against his head failed to discharge when the gunman pulled the trigger. The police believe the bandits had a silencer, as Auguste said he heard no report when his father was shot. Both holdup men fled when Auguste shouted for help and a pursuing patrolman lost them in the darkness."

According to the *Fall River Herald News*, "Police dogs used in the chase followed the men for two miles."

OUTCOME

Unsolved

AFTERWORD

Louis Chouinard's son, Auguste Chouinard, was the Fall River City Tax Collector at the time of his father's death.

FURTHER READING

"Nothing in Annals of Fall River Attracted As Much Attention as Borden Murder Case," *Fall River Herald News* (Fall River, Massachusetts), September 19, 1958.

"No Trace of Bandits Who Shot Merchant." *Hartford Courant* (Hartford, Connecticut), December 7, 1925.

MANUEL JOHN SANTOS

CRIME	Gun shot murder at the vacant 289 Montaup Street, in Fall River, Massachusetts, on September 27, 1926.
VICTIM	Manuel John Santos, 35
ACCUSED	Jan Kaminski, 52
DETAILS	Manuel John Santos was having a love affair with Mrs. Amelia Kaminski when her husband, Jan, shot them both after following them to a vacant room on Montaup Street in Fall River. Santos died on October 7. Amelia recovered.
THE TRIAL	Kaminski pleaded guilty to second-degree murder.
OUTCOME	On March 2, 1927, Jan Kaminski was given a life and one day term to spend in solitary confinement. Kaminski was pardoned on December 20, 1934, by Governor Joseph B. Ely of Massachusetts but he later violated his parole and was taken back to prison.
FURTHER READING	"Nothing in Annals of Fall River Attracted As Much Attention as Borden Murder Case," *Fall River Herald News* (Fall River, Massachusetts), September 19, 1958.

HELEN MACOMBER SHERMAN SHAW

CRIME

Husband shoots wife to death in their home in Mattapoisett, Massachusetts, and then commits suicide, on November 21, 1926.

VICTIM

Helen Macomber (Sherman) Shaw, wife, 46

ACCUSED

James Ebenezer Norton Shaw, husband, 50

DETAILS

J.E. Norton Shaw, a prominent New Bedford attorney, and former famous Harvard football athlete, in an apparent crisis over a probate court matter that was to be tried the following Monday and Tuesday, shot his wife and then himself, killing both.

According to the *Hartford Courant* (November 27, 1926), "Mrs. Catherine Sherman, housekeeper at the Shaw home … at about 5 o'clock this afternoon, Mr. Shaw took a gun he had in the house and remarked that he was going to shoot a rat. Mrs. Sherman saw Mr. Shaw go into the upper part of his house and in a few minutes she said she heard the explosion of the gun. Mrs. Sherman hurried into the second story of the house and there she saw Mr. Shaw standing in the middle of his wife's bedroom, and Mrs. Shaw was on the floor. 'My God,' exclaimed Mr. Shaw, 'I've shot my wife, go get a doctor.'

"Mrs. Sherman ran down stairs to the telephone and while she was calling up Dr. Tilden she heard another explosion and leaving the telephone she ran up stairs again and found Mr. Shaw was on the floor with blood streaming from a self inflicted wound. He was dead before help could be summoned.

"Mr. Shaw was an executor of the estate of George T. Russell, who died in Acushnet [Massachusetts] about five years ago. Russell left an estate of about $105,000, and the bequests by will amounted to about $100,000. Now the town of Acushnet and other beneficiaries are objecting to the allowance of the account. At the time the will was made there was sufficient funds in the estate to meet all the bequests. Mr. Russell died shortly after making the will. A few days prior to the death, there was withdrawn from the New Bedford Institution for Savings, more than $42,000. This was paid on orders signed by Mr. Russell, the major share of the amount withdrawn going to Mrs. Rebecca C. Holmes, it is alleged, and a smaller amount to J.E. Norton Shaw. Mrs. Holmes and Mr. Shaw were named executors in the will. It is their account that is being contested by the beneficiaries."

Local gossip has it that Russell had fallen for the much younger Rebecca (he was in his 60s and she was in her 20s). She declined his marriage proposal and later married Wallace Holmes. When she became pregnant, Russell supposedly offered her $40,000 to name the child after him, which she accepted. Unfortunately the boy child died as did Russell soon following.

Mrs Shaw was born Helen Macomber Sherman in October, 1880. Her father was William Bradford Sherman, died in 1924 at the age of 75, and her mother was Rosalinda Lewis (Cook) Sherman, died in 1936 at the age of 81. Helen attended Brown University and graduated in 1902. James and Helen were married in 1900. James earned his law degree from Harvard in 1901. They had no children. James was the son of Bruce Freeman and Eliza Angelia (Cook) Shaw of Mattapoisett.

At the inquest held in January of 1927, it was determined that Shaw had "deliberately shot and killed his wife and then committed suicide." Judge Nathan Washburn based his findings, says the *Fitchburg Sentinel*, "on the fact that Shaw was hopelessly entangled financially and facing a situation damaging to his reputation as a lawyer; that Mrs. Shaw would have been drawn into the matter as endorser of certain notes; that the shotgun used had been tested by an expert and found to be impossible of accidental discharge." The judge also said that "Mr. and Mrs. Shaw were a singularly devoted couple and there was not lack of harmony between them."

Initially, the medical examiner and investigating officials "declared themselves satisfied" that "accidental shooting and suicide" was the probable cause. According to the *Hartford Courant* (November 28, 1926), "They described as mere coincidence the fact that the shooting occurred on the eve of a probate court hearing in which Shaw was to have been questioned as to his conduct in connection with a will of which he as an executor. Dr. Raymond H. Baxter, associated medical examiner, who performed an autopsy on the bodies, announced that he would report accidental shooting and suicide in his findings. Mrs. Shaw was shot and killed by her husband, who explained that he had taken his shotgun to kill a rat. While a physician was being summoned to tend Mrs. Shaw, the lawyer turned the weapon on himself … In proof the fact that the attorney feared nothing from the probate court's inquiry, friends said today that after yesterday's conference in his office"

THE TRIAL

Since this was a murder/suicide, there was no trial, and the public was left to their intense speculation as to the motive for Shaw's actions in the tragedy.

AFTERWORD

It was thought by some that when J.E. Shaw said he was going upstairs to "shoot a rat" that he might have been referring to his wife, as she may have threatened to reveal some details of his questionable probate issue to the courts the following Monday.

FURTHER READING

"$105,000 Will Fight Pending As Shaw Kills Wife, Self." *The Brooklyn Daily Eagle* (Brooklyn, New York), November 27, 1926.

"Barnyard Rat Indirect Cause of Dual Tragedy." *The Evening News* (Harrisburg, Pennsylvania), November 27, 1926.

Decicco-Carey, Kyle. "The Shadows." southcoasthistory. wordpress.com. June 24, 2013.

"Finds Shaw Killed Wife and Self." *Fitchburg Sentinel* (Fitchburg, Massachusetts), January 21, 1927.

"Ex-Grid Star Kills Wife and Himself." *Hartford Courant* (Hartford, Connecticut), November 27, 1926.

"Ex-Grid Star Shot Wife, Inquest Finds." *The Bridgeport Telegram* (Bridgeport, Connecticut), January 22, 1927.

"Ex-Harvard Star in Dual Shooting." *The North Adams Transcript* (North Adams, Massachusetts), November 27, 1926.

"Killed Wife by Accident To Be Report." *Hartford Courant* (Hartford, Connecticut), November 28, 1926.

"Kills Wife in Gun Accident; Ends Own Life." *Chicago Daily Tribune* (Chicago, Illinois), November 27, 1926.

"Lawyer, Ex-Football Star Kills Wife and Himself." *The Morning News* (Wilmington, Delaware), November 27, 1926.

"Lawyer Slays Wife and Kills Himself; Worried Over Case." *The Philadelphia Inquirer* (Philadelphia, Pennsylvania), November 27, 1926.

"Shaw Murder Doubted." *The Philadelphia Inquirer* (Philadelphia, Pennsylvania), November 28, 1926.

"Woman Must Account for $81,000 Estate." *The Bridgeport Telegram* (Bridgeport, Connecticut), November 12, 1927.

GALLERY

The Shadows. 8 North Street, Mattapoisett, Massachusetts.

"James Ebenezer Norton Shaw, ca. 1898"
Image courtesy of the SouthCoastHistory.Wordpress.com.

"James Ebenezer Norton Shaw, ca. 1920"
Image courtesy of the SouthCoastHistory.Wordpress.com.

MARY MORIARTY

CRIME	Mary Moriarty and her husband, Edward, were shot at their home at 59 Union Street, in Fall River, Massachusetts, by the accused on January 27, 1927. Edward survived.
VICTIM	Mary Moriarty, 32
ACCUSED	Peter A. Dyer, 35

DETAILS

Mary Moriarty was a mother of two children. She was having an affair with the accused, who was a painter and paperhanger and the father of five. Her two sons, John, 7, and Edward, 5, were witnesses to the shooting in the kitchen. Edward was wounded but survived.

According to *The Courier-News*, the police reported that "Dyer confessed that he had been enamored of Mrs. Moriarty. In a jealous rage, police said, he went to the Moriarty home and, in the presence of the two Moriarty children killed the mother and wounded the father. Then he surrendered to police."

THE TRIAL

Peter A. Dyer was found guilty of first degree murder. On Marcy 9, 1927, Dyer received a sentence of life in prison.

OUTCOME

Dyer received a pardon on Thanksgiving Day 1935 from Governor James Curley. He violated his parole and was taken back to prison but released again in 1942, after serving seventeen years.

FURTHER READING

"Father of Five Murders Married Woman." *The Courier-News* (Bridgewater, New Jersey), January 29, 1927.
"Kills Woman and Shoots Husband in Quarrel Over Visits." *Reading Times* (Reading, Pennsylvania), January 29, 1927.
"Nothing in Annals of Fall River Attracted As Much Attention as Borden Murder Case," *Fall River Herald News* (Fall River, Massachusetts), September 19, 1958.

THEODORE GIBBONS

CRIME
Murder in East Swansea, Massachusetts, on April 23, 1927.

VICTIM
Theodore Gibbons, 26

ACCUSED
Mrs. Gertrude Franzer Gibbons, wife, and Antone Da Silva, her lover.

DETAILS
Mrs. Gertrude Gibbons was the young wife of mill worker Theodore Gibbons. According to *The Ithaca Journal*, Gibbons' body "was found ... in a well in East Swansea." She and Antone Da Silva, "with whom she was convicted last year on a statutory charge," were arrested for the murder of her husband, Theodore.

"Mrs. Gibbons' arrest came after a four-hour interrogation at police headquarters. She has previously been questioned by District Attorney William C. Crossley. Da Silva had been subjected to a searching cross-examination earlier in the day. Police assert they are in possession of the weapon which they believed had been used in the slaying. They refused to reveal its nature. Mrs. Gibbons, who is the mother a four-year-old son, had not lived with her husband recently.

"Gibbons had sued Da Silva for $3,000 for alienation of affections after the arrest of the couple last November and their subsequent conviction. Rudolphe Boulay of this city found Gibbons' body in a well on his Summer home. It was fully clothed and money and papers were undisturbed. The skull had been crushed, and the well cover had been weighted down with a rock."

According to *The Bridgeport Telegram*, Gibbons and Da Silva "were indicted for first degree murder and also for lewd and lascivious co-habitation by the Bristol county grand jury."

THE TRIAL

After a preliminary trial, the defendants were turned over to the Grand Jury. Da Silva could not understand English and was provided an interpreter.

Both Gertrude Gibbons and Da Silva pleaded not guilty to the charge of murdering Theodore Gibbons. Gertrude was acquitted of crushing her husband's skull. Da Silva was convicted.

OUTCOME

Da Silva was sent to Bridgewater State Hospital and then recalled and allowed to plead guilty to manslaughter on April 9, 1828. He was sentenced to seven to ten years. Da Silva was released from prison in April of 1935.

FURTHER READING

"Deny Murder Charges." *Hartford Courant* (Hartford, Connecticut), June 21, 1927.
"Nothing in Annals of Fall River Attracted As Much Attention as Borden Murder Case," *Fall River Herald News* (Fall River, Massachusetts), September 19, 1958.
"Pair Indicted for Killing Husband." *The Bridgeport Telegram* (Bridgeport, Connecticut), June 11, 1927.
"Sensational Murder Trial Starts in Fall River." *The Daily Free Press* (Carbondale, Illinois), November 28, 1927.
"2 Face Charge of Murdering Mill Worker." *The Ithaca Journal* (Ithaca, New York), May 24, 1927.

GALLERY

"Top photo is unusual picture of a murder trial defendant at scene of her alleged crime together with jury that will decide her fate. Mrs. Gertrude E. Gibbons (arrow, in hat, second person from the left) and jurors visit lonely South Swansea, Mass., farm and inspect well where Theodore Gibbons' body was discovered. Lower left: Mary August, Mrs. Gibbons' sister, snapped in court at trial. Lower right: Mrs. Gibbons confers with her counsel, Attorney Frank, planning defense in Fall River, Mass., courthouse." *The Daily Free Press*, November 28, 1927.

DALPHA PELLETIER

CRIME

Murder with a twelve gauge shotgun in a home on Viscombe Road, in Swansea, Massachusetts, on October 30, 1927.

VICTIM

Dalpha Pelletier, 23

ACCUSED

Elmer K. Pierce, 43

DETAILS

Elmer Pierce shot and killed Dalpha Pelletier while she was visiting Thelma Berard Pierce, his ex-wife. Pierce had been unsuccessful in multiple attempts to win her back. His earlier attempt to dynamite her house failed.

THE TRIAL

Elmer Pierce pleaded guilty to second-degree murder. The trial lasted less than fifteen minutes.

OUTCOME

On April 9, 1928, Elmer Pierce was sentenced to life and one day in solitary confinement in prison.

FURTHER READING

"New Bedford, Mass." *The Palm Beach Post* (West Palm Beach, Florida), April 10, 1928.
"Nothing in Annals of Fall River Attracted As Much Attention as Borden Murder Case," *Fall River Herald News* (Fall River, Massachusetts), September 19, 1958.

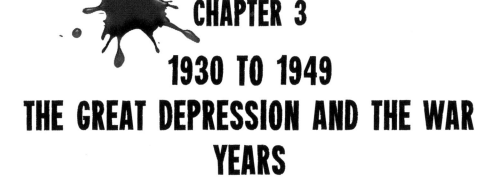

CHAPTER 3
1930 TO 1949
THE GREAT DEPRESSION AND THE WAR YEARS

Nine cotton manufacturing mills closed in Fall River in 1930 and the entire workforce was down 75% from 1924 totals. Thus began an economic decline from which the SouthCoast area has never recovered. By 1931, the Commonwealth of Massachusetts State Finance Board had assumed management of the City of Fall River and controlled its finances for a decade. In short order, the intense competition from the South saw an additional ten mills close and thousands lose their jobs and livelihoods.

New Bedford likewise saw a population decline during the same time, moving from an all-time high of 121,217 in 1920 to ten thousand people less a decade later. New Bedford's textile industry help to sustain its economic life when the whaling industry ended in 1925. But that also disappeared in the 1940s, to be replaced by commerical fishing, tourism, health care, and manufacturing.

The war years of the 1940s brought some prosperity to both communities, as wars often do, as orders for products picked up. The population in the metropolitan area of Fall River stabilized at 115,000 but would forever continue to decline from the all-time high of 120,000 in 1920. During the war years, many SouthCoasters went to see Carol Lombard in the movie *From Hell to Heaven*. Many others visited Mac Andrade's Latin Quarter Lounge to see Rose Marie and help break previous attendance records. With the end of Prohibition in 1933, beer and hard liquor once again became openly and widely consumed. Unfortunately, too many men overindulged with the result that many deaths connected to alcohol became part of the local landscape.

Yet still there were murders. The violence was driven by passion, greed, and grudges. Guns seemed to be the instrument of choice but knives and bare hands also played major roles in the slayings. Insanity continued to be blamed for many acts of mayhem and, in many cases, suicides were committed after the murders.

More lives were lost to violence during the Depression years, while during the war, as more lives were being taken abroad, at home, things had calmed.

The violence of the era was evident in the crimes: an eight-year old was killed by her uncle as the result of a grudge against her father, his brother-in law; a wife clubbed her husband to death; a woman was garroted by her neighbor. The most famous murder of the era was the Elliot "Pinky" Hathaway case, which resulted in the conviction of the upper-class man for the strangulation of a nursing student he had taken on a date. Her body was found draped on a stone farm wall nearby in Tiverton, Rhode Island. After his jail time was served, "Pinky" returned to live in the Fall River for many years until his death from natural causes.

It was also during this period that another major fire erupted in Fall River. In 1941, the main building of the old Print Works in Fall River on the Taunton River went up in flames. Tons of raw rubber were lost in the conflagration and the war effort suffered a major setback because the Firestone Rubber & Latex Company, Inc., was the leading producer of gas masks and other vital defense and military equipment. The local economy also suffered greatly with the loss of 2,600 jobs due to the blaze. Although the textile industry had pretty much departed from the area, there was an abundance of vacant factory space and an eager workforce. Enter the garment industry and the needle trades, both of which prospered until these sewing jobs went to the Asia and Central America. And so it goes.

HELEN NAJA

CRIME	Husband kills wife and then self in a murder/suicide at 33 Jesse Street, Fairhaven, Massachusetts, on January 4, 1930.
VICTIM	Helen Naja, 33
ACCUSED	Anthony Naja, 44

DETAILS

Anthony Naja, a war veteran, for some unknown reason, shot his wife and then himself, both lingering a day in the hospital until succumbing to their injuries. Before Anthony died, he was charged with murder.

"Chief Walter H. Francis of the Fairhaven police discovered the couple when he called at the house late Saturday afternoon. Anthony Naja was on the floor of the kitchen unconscious with a bullet wound in his head and gas flowing from the stove. His wife had run to the home of a neighbor where she collapsed" (*Hartford Courant*).

THE TRIAL

No trial as this was a murder/suicide.

FURTHER READING

"War Veteran Kills Wife, Shoots Self." *Hartford Courant* (Hartford, Connecticut), January 5, 1930.

JOSEPH KIRBY

CRIME

A man clubbed to death by his wife in their home at 198 Rockland Street, Fall River, Massachusetts, on December 16, 1930.

VICTIM

Joseph Kirby, 57

ACCUSED

Julia Kirby, 66

DETAILS

Julia Kirby killed her husband, Joseph, a slaubber tender in a Fall River textile mill, in their kitchen after a fight. When the chair she was sitting on broke, she used a chair leg to hit and kill him.

THE TRIAL

Julia Kirby was found guilty of manslaughter.

OUTCOME

Julia Kirby was sentenced to six years in Sherborn Reformatory for Women.

AFTERWORD

According to the *Dictionary of Occupational Titles*, a "subber tender" has many duties in a textile mill. They tend "slubber machines that draw out and loosely twist sliver into roving to strengthen sliver for subsequent drawing and twisting operations: Fastens ends of sliver from full cans to preceding ends by overlapping and twisting ends with fingers, or threads sliver over guide, through rolls and flyers, and onto bobbins. Patrols machines to detect exhausted ends and to observe signal lights indicating machine stoppage caused by sliver breaks. Pieces up broken ends by threading sliver through rollers and flyer and twisting sliver to end on bobbin. Doffs bobbin of roving, placing flyers on top of frame and roving in box truck. Sets empty bobbins on spindles, winds end of roving around bobbins, and replaces flyers. Brushes lint and dust from rollers and oils machine."

JOSEPHINE SLUSAK

CRIME

Man attempts to murder his wife and then commits suicide in Fall River, Massachusetts, on July 2, 1930.

VICTIM

Josephine Slusak, recovered, 29

ACCUSED

Max Repsky, former husband, 29

DETAILS

After shooting his divorced wife twice in the head and thinking her dead, Max Repsky elected to commit suicide by turning the gun on himself. Repsky and his ex-wife had been quarreling for some time. According to The *Ithaca Journal*, "Miss Slusak, who had been standing in conversation with three men when Repsky approached and opened fire, was taken to the same hospital as her former husband."

According to a report in the *Fitchburg Sentinel*, "Friends of the couple said that their disagreements started shortly after their marriage four years ago and led to a divorce six months ago. Repsky had not been seen hereabouts since the divorce until last Sunday. He was alleged to have made numerous threats against his former wife before he dropped out of sight, but his actions had not been unusual since his return."

Slusak survived her wounds.

THE TRIAL

No trial, as Repsky killed himself.

FURTHER READING

"Mill Hand Shoots his Divorced Wife." *The Ithaca Journal* (Ithaca, New York), July 2, 1930.
"Millhand Shoots His Divorced Wife, Self." *The Scranton Republican* (Scranton, Pennsylvania), July 3, 1930.
"Shoots Divorced Wife and Self at Fall River." *Fitchburg Sentinel* (Fitchburg, Massachusetts), July 2, 1930.
"Shoots Divorced Wife and Then Himself." *The News Journal* (Wilmington, Delaware), July 2, 1930.

VERNA RUSSELL

CRIME   A woman is murdered by strangulation and her body found in Winward Lane, off 270 Stafford Road, in Tiverton, Rhode Island, on March 23, 1931.

VICTIM   Verna Eloise Russell, 20, was a student nurse at Truesdale Hospital in Fall River, Massachusetts. She was born in Portland, Oregon, in September of 1910, and resided at the time of her death in Portsmouth, Rhode Island.

ACCUSED   Elliott Randall "Pinky" Hathaway, 28, the son of State Representative Louis E. Hathaway, was described as a lady's man, a womanizer, "a drug store cowboy," "the sheik with bottle of gin in his raccoon coat pocket," as well as a great basketball player in *The Durfee* (High School) *Record*.

DETAILS   Vernon V. Galvin, a friend of Elliott Hathaway, notified the Fall River police that Verna Russell had been killed and Hathaway had called "at his home about midnight, told him he had been riding with Miss Russell when two men armed with pistols ordered him to 'beat it,' and then attacked the girl. Hathaway then said he was going to 'get out of here,' and left, according to Galvin's story to the police" (*The Burlington Free Press*, March 25, 1931). A warrant was issued for Elliott Hathaway's arrest as the medical examiner determined that Russell had not been the victim of a criminal assault, but had been strangled. Hathaway gave himself up at the Hickson Hotel in North Attleboro, Massachusetts, and was arraigned in Newport District Court on a first degree murder charge. His car was discovered abandoned, sans slipcovers, on Beacon Hill in Boston, near the home of Hathaway's uncle, on March 24.

The medical examiner determined that the condition of Russell's body included contusions of the face, discolorations of the neck, with a missing upper right lateral incisor. He also discovered some silver from a tooth in the "fringe of the epiglottis." It became Hathaway's defense that the tooth had caused Russell to choke to death instead of her being the victim of strangulation. The medical experts disagreed, saying that the strangulation came "from human hands." There had been no sexual assault.

Galvin later testified that Hathaway told him how he had stuck Russell in a rage during an argument, after she told Hathaway she was engaged. This second story was told to Galvin the night of the killing when Hathaway drove him to the scene of the crime and pointed the body out to him.

THE TRIAL

According to a news article in the *Reno Gazette-Journal*, Hathaway testified that Verna Russell "died in his arms while they were engaged in a 'petting party' and drinking gin ... he did not know what happened. He had just handed the girl a bottle of ginger ale for use with the gin they were drinking when he heard the bottle fall to the floor of the automobile in which they were parked. He then heard a choking sound and a 'gurgling' noise and saw the girl clutch her throat with both hands ... Miss Russell 'fell over' and that he supported her with his arms, fanned her with his hat and tried other methods of resuscitation in vain. 'I could not understand it,' he said. 'I thought she had passed out from drinking alcohol.' He said he took the nurse from the rear seat of his automobile because he thought the air might revive her."

From the *Newport Mercury* (June 26, 1931), we learn that Hathaway then testified, "I got her out of the car and walked five feet with her. She seemed very heavy. I saw some grass and put her on it." The newspaper continues: "He tried working her arms, as he had seen it done on the football field. Felt of her heart; found no beating. Tried the pulse; there was no pulse. He was 10 minutes working over her, not feeling sure she was dead; he thought probably it was the effect of the alcohol she had taken. He started away, went as far as Stafford road. Stopped; walked back; tried again to revive her. She seemed dead. He sat down for 20 minutes or half an hour. Then he drove to 'Chick' Galvin's house. Went in. Told him to get his mother. Said, 'The girl has passed out on me; come back with me ... I did not say [to Galvin] I hit her, or that we had an argument over an interne [sic]. I did not mention an interne [sic].'

"Then when he started away, he halted his car on the main road, he said, and returned to try to aid her. He denied having told Vernon Galvin, the state's star witness and his own school-day friend, that he hit the girl in an argument, over an interne [sic] she intended to marry, as Galvin had testified Hathaway told him. It was their first 'date,' Hathaway said, but they had become friendly, stopping for kissing and drinks en route to the lonely lane."

The trial lasted three weeks and the jury took only seven minutes to vote Elliott Hathaway guilty of murder in the first degree. They said they believed that Hathaway was in the process of attempting to rape Miss Russell when he reacted to her refusal to engage in sex.

OUTCOME

Hathaway was given the mandatory life sentence for the first degree strangulation murder of Verna Russell. He was sent to Howard Prison in Cranston, Rhode Island, to serve his sentence.

AFTERWORD

In 1952, after twenty-one years in prison, Hathaway was denied parole. A year later, however, parole was granted "with the understanding that Hathaway live in another state other than Rhode Island or Massachusetts. Hathaway had asked to return to his aged mother" (*Newport Mercury*, September 11, 1953).

Hathaway moved to New Orleans and for the next twenty-four years worked in the oil business. He moved back to Fall River to care for his twin brother, Alden. He lived in the family house at 32 June Street, near the local YMCA where he remained until his death at age 81 on June 6, 1984.

ADDENDUM

It was of the utmost importance to investigators and the court to determine the exact location of Verna Russell's death. If she was found to have been killed in Massachusetts, and Hathaway had been found guilty, he would face the death penalty. Rhode Island did not have the same punishment for murder. Interestingly, Verna Russell's body was found on the Winward Estate, the site of the 1985 murder of Margaret Winward.

FURTHER READING

"Arranged Date for Hathaway." *The Burlington Free Press* (Burlington, Vermont), June 17, 1931.

"Ask Hathaway Verdict Set Aside." *Newport Mercury* (Newport, Rhode Island), July 19, 1931.

"Authorities Exhume Body for Pictures." *The Palm Beach Post* (West Palm Beach, Florida), April 28, 1931.

"Claim Death Caused by Heart Attack." *Newport Mercury* (Newport, Rhode Island), May 8, 1931.

"Claim Death From Natural Causes." *Newport Mercury* (Newport, Rhode Island), June 26, 1931.

"Death of Nurse is Described by Accused Youth." *Reno Gazette-Journal* (Reno, Nevada), June 23, 1931.

"Defense Starts in the Hathaway Case." *Newport Mercury* (Newport, Rhode Island), June 26, 1931.

"Dr. Peaslee Agrees with Dr. Bryant." *Newport Mercury* (Newport, Rhode Island), June 19, 1931.

"Doctors Support Hathaway's Alibi." *The Morning News* (Wilmington, Delaware), June 25, 1931.

"Fall River Man Surrenders in Murder Case." *The Portsmouth Herald* (Portsmouth, New Hampshire), March 26, 1931.

"Hathaway At Work in Jail Shirt Shop." *Newport Mercury* (Newport, Rhode Island), April 3, 1931.

"Hathaway Denies Killing Verna Russell." *The Burlington Free Press* (Burlington, Vermont), June 23, 1931.

"Hathaway Granted Parole in '31 County Murder Case." *Newport Mercury* (Newport, Rhode Island), September 11, 1953.

"Hathaway Guilty in First Degree." *Newport Mercury* (Newport, Rhode Island), July 3, 1931.

"Hathaway in Fall River at Time of Murder." *Newport Mercury* (Newport, Rhode Island), April 3, 1931.

"Hathaway in Prison Cell." *The Portsmouth Herald* (Portsmouth, New Hampshire), March 27, 1931.

"Hathaway Loses First Bid for Parole From Prison." *Newport Daily News* (Newport, Rhode Island), July 25, 1952.

"Hathaway Must Explain Things." *Newport Mercury* (Newport, Rhode Island), June 26, 1931.

"Hathaway Shows Court How He Lifted Nurse Out of His Automobile." *Fitchburg Sentinel* (Fitchburg, Massachusetts), June 23, 1931.

"Hathaway Takes Stand Today." *The Burlington Free Press* (Burlington, Vermont), June 22, 1931.

"Hunt Suspect In Death of Student Nurse." *Hartford Courant* (Hartford, Connecticut), March 26, 1931.

"More Evidence on Hathaway." *The Burlington Free Press* (Burlington, Vermont), June 19, 1931.

"Mother Helps Fight for Life." *Stevens Point Daily Journal* (Stevens Point, Wisconsin), June 29, 1931.

"Nothing in Annals of Fall River Attracted As Much Attention as Borden Murder Case," *Fall River Herald News* (Fall River, Massachusetts), September 19, 1958.

"Special Grand Jury Session Undecided." *Newport Mercury* (Newport, Rhode Island), April 3, 1931.

"Speculation As To Scene of Slaying." *Newport Mercury* (Newport, Rhode Island), April 3, 1931.

"Star Witness Takes Stand for State." *Newport Mercury* (Newport, Rhode Island), June 19, 1931.

"Young Woman Foully Slain." *The Burlington Free Press* (Burlington, Vermont), March 25, 1931.

GALLERY

"Where the body was found." *Hartford Courant*, March 26, 1931.

"Elliott R. Hathaway (right) of Fall River, Mass., arrested yesterday on a warrant charging him with the murder of Verna Russell (left), student nurse, whose body was found in a lonely land at Tiverton, RI. Hathaway had accompanied her on an auto ride prior to the finding of her body." *Burlington Free Press*, March 27, 1931.

"Fighting for his life at Newport, R.I., where he is on trial for the murder of pretty twenty-year-old Verna Russell, student nurse, Elliott R. Hathaway, son of Representative Louis Hathaway, of Massachusetts, is shown above with his mother during a court recess before the accused youth took the stand in his own defense." *Stevens Point Daily Journal*, June 29, 1931.

JOHN D. MCKINNON

CRIME	Murder by stabbing with a bread knife in Fall River, Massachusetts, on August 21, 1931.
VICTIM	John D. McKinnon, 37
ACCUSED	Louis Ramos, 33

DETAILS

In an apparent quarrel over a woman, John McKinnon, an oiler on tankers, and Louis Ramos engaged in an altercation that resulted in the death of McKinnon. Ramos took a taxi from the Flint section of the city to the South End and, possessing a lead pipe and a bread knife, stabbed the victim and left him for dead in an alley. Ramos was arrested because James Sumner, the 22-year-old son of Mrs. Clytie Sumner, McKinnon's landlady and the object of the quarrel, told police of the fight between the oiler and Ramos.

When serving in the Merchant Marines or on commercial tankers at sea, McKinnon went by the name of John McKenna.

THE TRIAL

Ramos was committed to the State Hospital for the Criminally Insane in Bridgewater, MA, and he remained there for sixteen years.

OUTCOME

In 1947, after his release from Bridgewater Hospital, Ramos was finally arraigned for manslaughter in the death of McKinnon and given a two-year sentence in the House of Correction.

FURTHER READING

"Fall River Man Faces Trial for 1931 Slaying." *The Berkshire Eagle* (Pittsfield, Massachusetts), September 11, 1947.
"Held for Mass. Slaying." *The News Journal* (Wilmington, Delaware), August 19, 1931.
"Jail Slayer." *Lebanon Daily News* (Lebanon, Pennsylvania), August 19, 1931.

HASKON OLSEN

CRIME	Drunk driver kills young sailor in Somerset, Massachusetts, on February 29, 1932.
VICTIM	Haskon Olsen, 21
ACCUSED	Alfred Roderick, 27

DETAILS

After drinking all evening, Alfred Roderick of South Dighton, Massachusetts, was involved in a hit and run on Route 138 in Somerset on the Dighton border. He killed a young Swedish Merchant Marine who was returning to his ship, the Norwegian freighter *Lampas*, that was docked at the Montaup Electric site in Somerset. Roderick was charged with leaving the scene of the accident until police found his brother's banged up truck that he had used at a local repair shop on County Street in Somerset.

THE TRIAL

Roderick was found guilty of drunk driving in the death of the sailor.

OUTCOME

He was sentenced to six months in jail and a cash fine of $600.

FURTHER READING

"Hit, Run Victim Dies." *Hartford Courant* (Hartford, Connecticut), Marcy 4, 1932.

ANNE MARIE GAUTHIER

CRIME	John Canuel and friend, Peter Luke Vailancourt, were accused of garroting a neighbor in Fall River, Massachusetts, on June 16, 1932.
VICTIM	Anne Marie Gauthier, 46
ACCUSED	John Canuel, 37, and Peter Luke Vailancourt, 43
DETAILS	Anne Marie Gauthier, a housekeeper, was strangled by her two neighbors on Wade Street in the Corky Row section of Fall River when they were looking for money to buy moonshine. They placed her body between two mattresses in her bedroom and left her.
THE TRIAL	Canuel pleaded guilty to the murder.
OUTCOME	Canuel confessed and was sentenced to life in state prison. Vailancourt was adjudged innocent and set free. Canuel went to jail and fifteen years later requested and was granted a pardon in 1947.
GALLERY	

Left: Peter Luke Vailancourt.
Right: John Canuel

ARTHUR AND MARILLA PELLETIER

CRIME

Husband and wife shot and killed in their living room on Gadoury Street, in North Westport, Massachusetts, on July 1, 1932.

VICTIMS

Arthur, husband, 24, and Marilla Pelletier, wife, 23

ACCUSED

Arthur Brown Manchester, 24

DETAILS

Arthur Manchester, a former boarder and farm hand at the Pelletier home in North Westport, broke into the Pelletier home on July 1, 1932, and, as the couple rose from bed and came into the living room, shot them both dead. The Pelletier's three-year-old son was asleep in his bed during the attack. The victims were discovered by Marilla's brother, Lucien Morreau, who found a screened window forced.

Arthur Manchester surrendered to police and confessed without providing a motive. When he was arraigned in district court on July 2, he pleaded not guilty and was held without bail for a hearing on July 14.

The murder weapon had been left with Manchester's cousin, Clarence Manchester, of Westport. According to *The Evening Journal*, "Officers went to [Clarence Manchester's] home and found the gun a .38 caliber revolver and Manchester subsequently identified it, police said."

THE TRIAL

After confessing to the crime, he was indicted on two counts of murder. He was found guilty and was ordered executed.

OUTCOME

The execution was to take place during the week of September 10, 1933, but the sentence was commuted to life imprisonment.

FURTHER READING

"Hold Alleged Slayer of Westport Couple." *Fitchburg Sentinel* (Fitchburg, Massachusetts), July 2, 1932.

"Say Farm Hand Has Confessed Double Murder." *The Evening Journal* (Wilmington, Delaware), July 2, 1932.

"Young Couple Slain as They Arise from Bed." *The Evening News* (Wilkes-Barre, Pennsylvania), July 1, 1932.

GUSSIE STONE

CRIME
Intoxicated husband shoots his wife to death and then turns the gun on himself, committing suicide, at 261 Bedford Street, in Fall River, Massachusetts, on July 28, 1933.

VICTIM
Gussie Stone, 48

ACCUSED
Harry Stone, 44

DETAILS
In the heat of a marital argument in their Bedford Street rooming house in Fall River, Harry Stone shot his wife six times and then turned the gun on himself. Their son, David, had drowned two years prior and left both parents bereft. According to reports, Harry had been drinking heavily.

FURTHER READING
"Nothing in Annals of Fall River Attracted As Much Attention as Borden Murder Case," *Fall River Herald News* (Fall River, Massachusetts), September 19, 1958.

STANLEY CYRON

CRIME

During a fight, one man is killed after being thrown down a flight of stairs in Fall River, Massachusetts, on July 7, 1933.

VICTIM

Stanley Cyron, 42

ACCUSED

Wojciech Kascia, 55

DETAILS

Stanley Cyron and Wojciech Kascia had been drinking for some time. A fight apparently broke out and Cyron was thrown down a flight of stone stairs, fracturing his skull. He died soon afterwards.

THE TRIAL

Wojciech Kascia, whose first name means "he who enjoys war" in Polish, was charged with manslaughter.

OUTCOME

Wojciech Kascia was found guilty of manslaughter and sentenced to two and a half years in prison.

MATTO RAZZA

CRIME

During an argument that led to a fight, a barber shoots and kills an Italian immigrant on Bedford Street, between Twelfth and Robeson Streets, in Fall River, Massachusetts, on August 19, 1934.

VICTIM

Matto Razza aka Razzio, 36

ACCUSED

Emilio DeCiccio, 53

DETAILS

Matto Razza, an Italian immigrant, was shot late at night after a scuffle with Emilio DeCiccio, owner of Modern Barber Shop on Bedford Street. They had been drinking together at a local restaurant until 10 p.m. A third man held the victim's arms behind his back during the scuffle. The gun involved in the shooting was found fifteen feet away from the body. Razza had a long police record in Providence, Rhode Island. In fact, the 1930 Federal Census shows him as a prisoner in the State Prison of Rhode Island in Cranston.

THE TRIAL

On November 9, 1935, Emilio DeCiccio was indicted on second-degree murder in a Taunton, Massachusetts, court.

OUTCOME

DeCiccio pleaded guilty to manslaughter and was sentenced to five to ten years in state prison.

FURTHER READING

"Identify Man Believed Slain in Fall River." *Fitchburg Sentinel* (Fitchburg, Massachusetts), August 20, 1934.
"Nothing in Annals of Fall River Attracted As Much Attention as Borden Murder Case," *Fall River Herald News* (Fall River, Massachusetts), September 19, 1958.

LOUIS LAROCHELLE

CRIME	Man shot and killed attempting to thwart a hold-up on Globe Street, in Fall River, Massachusetts, on September 18, 1937.
VICTIM	Louis LaRochelle, 53
ACCUSED	Tadrus Makara, 21, Gene Burns, 21, and Stephen Tarsa, 24
DETAILS	Tadrus Makara, Gene Burns, and Stephen Tarsa, all with lengthy criminal records, attempted to rob the St. Denis Liquor Store, 818 Globe Street, in Fall River. LaRochelle was a clerk in the liquor store. He was shot near the heart and died. The bandits made off with a bottle of gin.
THE TRIAL	Tarsa confessed that he was the "trigger man" and implicated both Burns and Makara. The trio was charged with second-degree murder.
OUTCOME	Makara, Burns and Tarsa all pleaded guilty to second-degree murder and were sentenced to life in prison and solitary confinement.
AFTERWORD	Makara died in prison. Governor Paul Dever pardoned Burns in 1951, and Tarsa was pardoned in January of 1953.

FURTHER READING

"Admits Shooting at Murder Trial." *The North Adams* Transcript (North Adams, Massachusetts), March 12, 1938.
"Nothing in Annals of Fall River Attracted As Much Attention as Borden Murder Case," *Fall River Herald News* (Fall River, Massachusetts), September 19, 1958.
"Fall River." *Fitchburg Sentinel* (Fitchburg, Massachusetts), March 11, 1938.
"Three Get Life Terms." *The Lincoln Star* (Lincoln, Nebraska), Marcy 13, 1938.

CECILA DAREGO

CRIME

Wife stabbed and killed by her ex-husband at 355 Snell Street, in Fall River, Massachusetts, on April 22, 1939.

VICTIM

Cecila daRego, 25

ACCUSED

Stephen W. Tolentino, 41 (Estevao Gustave Tolentino)

DETAILS

Stephen Tolentino, a Cape Verdian textile mill operator, had been estranged from his wife for some time. On April 22, 1939, Tolentino visited daRego at her residence, their former abode, and stabbed her to death with a stiletto fashioned from a carpenter's key-hole saw, which severed her left jugular vein.

According to *The Pittsburgh Press*, "Manuel Andrade, 36, of Freetown, was in another room listening to a radio, told police Mr. Tolentino came out of the bedroom and said: 'I've done it. I've done it. It's all over. You can go home now.' When Mr. Andrade walked to the door of the bedroom, he said he saw Mrs. Tolentino [his estranged wife] lying on the floor, her clothing disheveled. Then he telephoned police."

Tolentino was arrested and held without bail. According to *The Portsmouth Herald*, "District Attorney William C. Crossley told Judge Benjamin Cook that he wished to investigate several angles of the case, including the defendant's alleged confession that he had planned to slay several other persons."

THE TRIAL

Tolentino had made a complete and signed confession and wanted to plead guilty but had been advised by his lawyer that the offense was a capital crime for which he could be executed and he should plead not guilty.

OUTCOME

On November 23, 1939, Tolentino was sentenced to prison for life. The 1940 Federal Census showed that he was residing at the State Prison of Massachusetts in Boston.

FURTHER READING

"Held in Slaying." *The Daily Courier* (Connellsville, Pennsylvania), April 26, 1939.

"Nothing in Annals of Fall River Attracted As Much Attention as Borden Murder Case," *Fall River Herald News* (Fall River, Massachusetts), September 19, 1958.

"Pleads Innocent to Murder Charge." *The Portsmouth Herald* (Portsmouth, New Hampshire), April 24, 1939.

"Wife Found Slain, Mill Operator Held." *The Pittsburgh Press* (Pittsburgh, Pennsylvania), April 23, 1939.

GALLERY

Left: Cecelia da Rego. Right: Stephen Tolentino

IRENE PERRY

CRIME

Young unwed mother found garroted, trussed with ropes, and left on a wooded road in Dartmouth, Massachusetts, on June 29, 1940.

VICTIM

Irene Perry, 22

ACCUSED

Frank Pedro, 25

DETAILS

According to Perry's brother, John, Irene had left home in a happy mood on June 29, 1940, to pay a bill at a clothing store and get some ice cream for her 2-year-old son, Donald, and had not returned. Police determined that she had paid the bill and made some additional purchases. Irene was one of twelve children and was the "mother" of her siblings. Her father, Joseph, was a greenskeeper at the New Bedford Country Club. When her mother died, Irene had left the seventh grade to care for her eight sisters and four brothers.

Her body was discovered a month later.

According to the *Pittsburgh Press*, a berry-picking "WPA worker Henry de Salves yesterday saw what he thought was a sack under a low-hanging pine tree. The 'sack' was the girl's dress [red and white checked], drawn over her head and knotted. It was 25 yards from an old timber road. The spot was so isolated that it was five hours before police could remove the body to town. The body lay on an auto floor mat, the arms crossed in such a way that the hands covered the mouth. Two strands of heavy hemp rope constricted the throat. One of the girl's stockings had been removed and used to bind her ankles. The dress and coat had been pulled over her head and tied like a flower bag. An autopsy discovered that Irene was an expectant mother, and it was learned that she had given birth to a son three years ago." Police believed that she had been killed in another location, perhaps nearby, and then dragged to the spot beneath the tree after death. The nearest automobile tracks were 200 yards away.

Police first thought they had the killer, a 31-year-old New Bedford mill-hand, who they questioned throughout the night of the discovery of the body, but they released him after checking out his alibi, admitting that they were without a clue to a new suspect.

Irene had told friends that she knew she was pregnant and was engaged to marry a man from Fall River. "Efforts were begun to learn the identity of the Fall River man and to trace a ring he was said to have given her. The ring was missing when the girl's body, trussed with rope, was found near an old timber road by WPA workers. Police checked jewelry stores in southeastern Massachusetts on the theory that the man might have purchased the ring on installments, in which case he would have had to give his name and that of the person for whom it was intended (*The Daily Republican*). This line of inquiry was abandoned when it was learned that Irene had been joking when she told friends that she was engaged. The ring was found in her room.

Frank Pedro of South First Street in New Bedford, a married father of one child and a former farm worker in Portsmouth, pleaded not guilty to first degree murder. He was held without bail for trial in September. The police maintained that "the rope with which the girl was strangled and with her hands were tied above her head was traced through the manufacture to a Portsmouth farm where Pedro had been employed building a silo. Chief Brownell said similar rope was found at the farm and also at Pedro's home. He said that accused man was friendly with the girl and was seen with her on numerous occasions" (*Newport Mercury*).

THE TRIAL

The trial of Frank Pedro for the murder of Irene Perry was held in May of 1941. A rope expert testified for the defense that the rope found in Pedro's cellar was not, as the prosecution asserted, of the same manufacture and type as the rope which bound the body of Irene Perry. Reports the *Fitchburg Sentinel*, "Andrew Landini, Littleton chemist, testified that the rope found on the body was manufactured by the Cating Rope works, of New York, and said that an analysis of the rope dressing used in that plant revealed it contained 38 per cent rosin. Analysis of the rope found in Pedro's cellar showed no trace of rosin, he said."

During the trial, the jury visited the location where Irene Perry's body was discovered.

Frank Pedro was found not guilty. After his acquittal, he returned to his home in New Bedford and his wife Odelia and son Frank, Jr.

OUTCOME

Irene Perry's case remains unsolved.

FURTHER READING

"Dispute Report on Rope in Pedro Murder Trial." *Fitchburg Sentinel* (Fitchburg, Massachusetts), May 26, 1941.

"Former Portsmouth Farm Worker Held." *Newport Mercury* (Newport, Rhode Island), August 30, 1940.

"Girl Found Garroted in Lover's Lane." *The Daily Republican* (Monongahela, Pennsylvania), August 1, 1940.

"Girl, 22, Found Slain in Forest." *Bradford Evening Star and The Bradford Daily Record* (Bradford, Pennsylvania), August 1, 1940.

"Laborer Accused in Murder." *The Hartford Courant* (Hartford, Connecticut), August 28, 1940.

"Man Pleads Innocent to Murder Charge." *Fitchburg Sentinel* (Fitchburg, Massachusetts), September 7, 1940.

"Missing Woman is Found Slain." *The Monroe News-Star* (Monroe, Louisiana), August 1, 1940.

"New Bedford Man Held On Charge of Murder." *Fitchburg Sentinel* (Fitchburg, Massachusetts), August 20, 1940.

"Police Check Five Alibis in Murder of Dartmouth Girl." *Dunkirk Evening Observer* (Dunkirk, New York), August 2, 1940.

"Unwed Mother Found Slain in Woods Off 'Lovers' Lane.'" *Asbury Park Press* (Asbury Park, New Jersey), August 1, 1940.

"Woman Strangled; No Clew to Killer." *St. Louis Post-Dispatch* (St. Louis, Missouri), August 1, 1940.

"Young 'Mother' of 12 is Killed." *The Pittsburgh Press* (Pittsburgh, Pennsylvania), August 1, 1940.

GALLERY

Irene Perry. *St. Louis Post-Dispatch*, August 1, 1940.

JAMES GEANECOPOULAOS

CRIME

Victim bludgeoned and robbed of $1,400 from the sale of chickens at his home on Padelford Street, in Berkley, Massachusetts, on April 15, 1943.

VICTIM

James Geanecopoulaos, 48

ACCUSED

George Curtiss, 69

DETAILS

James Geanecopoulaos, a Greek immigrant, was an unmarried farmer who was beaten to death and robbed of $1400 from a recent sale of chickens—the proceedings of which he planned to use to go on vacation. He was killed in his home without a struggle after Curtiss came to his house to allegedly borrow a tool. It was believed that the victim's dogs did not bark because they were familiar with the accused.

THE TRIAL

George Curtiss was tried in New Bedford and declared innocent by reason of insanity. He was sent to the Bridgewater State Hospital for life.

FURTHER READING

"Nothing in Annals of Fall River Attracted As Much Attention as Borden Murder Case," *Fall River Herald News* (Fall River, Massachusetts), September 19, 1958.

GALLERY

James Geanecopoulaos.

JOHN PURCELL

CRIME

Man knocked down and robbed while walking home, at Cherry and Purchase Streets, in Fall River, Massachusetts, in the evening of April 15, 1943.

VICTIM

John Purcell, 47

ACCUSED

Frank Amaral, Jr., 19, and Edmund Mello, 25

DETAILS

John Purcell was knocked down and robbed and his skull was fractured while walking home from his job as manager of a liquor store.

THE TRIAL

After being convicted of second degree murder, Amaral accused Mello of being an accomplice. Mello was tried and found guilty as well.

OUTCOME

Amaral was given life in prison. Mello was also given a life sentence five years later in 1952. The judge imposed a minimum thirty year sentence for the crime.

AFTERWORD

Purcell left two daughters, Lucille, 13 , and Joan, 7, and a wife, Marie Blanche, 38.

FURTHER READING

"Nothing in Annals of Fall River Attracted As Much Attention as Borden Murder Case," *Fall River Herald News* (Fall River, Massachusetts), September 19, 1958.

GALLERY

John Purcell.

EUGENIA OLIVEIRA

CRIME

Fiancé strangles wife-to-be on Pleasant Street in Fall River, Massachusetts, on October 21, 1947.

VICTIM

Eugenia Oliveira, 43

ACCUSED

Joseph W. Sylvia, 45

DETAILS

Joseph Sylvia and Eugenia Oliveira had made plans for a November wedding but a quarrel developed over her attention to other men. Sylvia strangled Oliveira to death with a child's jump rope and then attempted suicide by consuming ammonia. This act was unsuccessful.

THE TRIAL

Joseph Sylvia was convicted of first degree murder.

OUTCOME

On February 24, 1948, Silvia was sentenced to life imprisonment.

FURTHER READING

"Nothing in Annals of Fall River Attracted As Much Attention as Borden Murder Case," *Fall River Herald News* (Fall River, Massachusetts), September 19, 1958.

THERESA LAFLEUR

CRIME	Strangulation murder of a child by her uncle in Fall River, Massachusetts, on August 4, 1947.
VICTIM	Theresa LaFleur, 8
ACCUSED	Charles McGarty, 25, uncle

DETAILS

Charles McGarty was Veronica LaFleur's brother who maintained a grudge against Theresa's father. When Veronica's husband, Leo LaFleur, asked where his daughter was, McGarty, the dishonorably discharged Navy veteran, responded; "I killed her, so what?"

The LaFleur's lived at 62 Quarry Street, in Fall River.

The eight-year-old Theresa, the second oldest of five children in her family, was beaten and choked to death and her body left in [a] ... section of the Watuppa Freight Shed on Rodman Street. Her body was found after a four-hour search.

"Veteran police, according to Lieutenant Michael P. Ryan, were shocked by the condition in which they found the child's body early today after being guided by the uncle to a wooded section where it had been concealed in the brush. She had been missing overnight" (*Hartford Courant*).

Later reports called the case a "rape-slaying."

McGarty was a "reformatory parolee" who had been released a year previously after serving eleven months of two concurrent five year sentences for larceny and robbery of an automobile. Says the *Hartford Courant*, "Usually serving of 30 months of such a sentence is necessary to release, but the board said McCarty's record was good and members of his family had asked his release that he might support his ill mother."

THE TRIAL

Charles A. McGarty pleaded not guilty at his trial and denied under direct examination that he had confessed to the police that he had killed the child.

According the *Fitchburg Sentinel* (February 20, 1948), McGarty, at his trial, said, "'I was sleepy,' he testified, 'and wanted to get it over. I would have admitted anything to get out of police headquarters.' He said under cross examination, however, that he recalled meeting Theresa and taking her for a walk to ... the Fall River freight yard. 'What happened on the hill?' asked Dist. Atty. J. Edward Lajoie. 'I don't remember,' McGarty replied. 'I think I grabbed her by the throat. I don't know. I'm trying to remember.' He said he had been drinking for three or four days before his niece was slain. 'He frequently replied 'I don't remember' or 'I haven't any recollection of that' under direct examination. A picture of the girl's body was on the stenographer's table directly in front of the witness stand as McGarty began to testify. He averted his eyes for several minutes and then leaned over and turned it face down. Lajoie introduced evidence showing McGarty was given a bad conduct discharge from the navy after three years of service."

McCarty was convicted on February 27, 1948, of first degree murder and sentenced to death in the electric chair on the second jury ballot. The sentence was commuted to life in prison that made him eligible for parole after fifteen years.

OUTCOME

McGarty was sentenced to life in prison at Walpole State Prison in Massachusetts and was named one of the leaders of a prison riot in 1952 on Thanksgiving eve.

AFTERWORD

In 1949, a federal court order was issued that blocked the execution for two weeks. "William C. Crossley, attorney for McGarty, requested the writ on the ground his client was denied constitutional rights when state courts refused a defense request that he be subjected to psychiatric tests during his trial" (*Nashua Telegraph*).

After eleven reprieves and a call for a new trial during the three and a half years since he was convicted, Charles McGarty's sentence was commuted in 1951 by the Governor's Executive Council. It was reported in the

Fitchburg Sentinel (July 19, 1951) that only seven of the Governor's Council were present at the meeting, which approved the commutation, against the advice of the attorney general and parole board, without a recorded vote. One councilor charged the Governor Paul A. Dever with taking advantage of the absence of another member who would have opposed the request.

ADDENDUM

Veronica LaFleur, Theresa's mother, later went on record as opposed to the death penalty in Massachusetts during the height of the capital punishment debate in the late 1940s. She wrote a letter which was read in the Massachusetts Senate in 1949 during the debate on bills to modify the Massachusetts law which made execution the mandatory sentence in cases where the conviction was of first degree murder. The bills were defeated.

Her letter read, in part, "Although it was my child I do not wish to see my brother go to the chair. If he does, I, that child's mother, will not feel justice has triumphed" (*The Portsmouth Herald*, March 30, 1949).

FURTHER READING

"Charles McGarty." *Fitchburg Sentinel* (Fitchburg, Massachusetts), July 19, 1951.

"Charles McGarty Must Die in Electric Chair." *The North Adams Transcript* (North Adams, Massachusetts), June 8, 1949.

"Choked to Death Climax to Quarrel." *The Delphos Courant* (Delphos, Ohio), August 6, 1947.

"Court Order Blocks Death, Charles McGarty." *Nashua Telegraph* (Nashua, New Hampshire), June 30, 1949.

"Fall River Man's Execution Halted." *The North Adams Transcript* (North Adams, Massachusetts), June 30, 1949.

"Judge Dismissed New Trial Plea of Tot's Slayer." *The Portsmouth Herald* (Portsmouth, New Hampshire), July 28, 1949.

"McGarty's Case to Reach Jury Before Nightfall." *Fitchburg Sentinel* (Fitchburg, Massachusetts), Feb 20, 1948.

"Mother Opposes Penalty on Child's Rape-Slayer." *The Portsmouth Herald* (Portsmouth, New Hampshire), March 30, 1949.

"New Stay Granted McGarty in Slaying." *The Berkshire County Eagle* (Pittsfield, Massachusetts), November 14, 1950.

"Nothing in Annals of Fall River Attracted As Much Attention as Borden Murder Case," *Fall River Herald News* (Fall River, Massachusetts), September 19, 1958.

"Slayer McGarty Gets New Stay." *Berkshire County Eagle* (Pitts-field, Massachusetts), August 9, 1949.

"Uncle Held in Slaying of 8-Years-Old Niece." *Hartford Courant* (Hartford, Connecticut), August 6, 1947.

GALLERY

McGarty hides face as detectives question him.

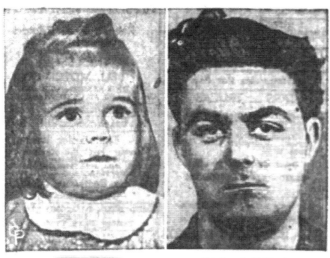

Theresa LaFleur   Charles A. McGarty

JOHN A. O'BRIEN

CRIME

Man shot his friend in the head and then turned the gun on himself at 303 Fifth Street, in Fall River, Massachusetts, on January 11, 1948.

VICTIM

John A. O'Brien, 30

ACCUSED

John P. Manning, Jr., 23

DETAILS

John O'Brien and John P. Manning were neighbors and long-time friends in the Corky Row section of Fall River. After a night of drinking, which Manning wanted to continue, an argument ensued and Manning shot and killed O'Brien while he was sitting in a leather chair in Manning's downstairs apartment. O'Brien was stuck behind the left ear and Manning was wounded critically after being shot near the right temple with a .38 caliber revolver, which was found on the floor of the apartment.

Police Captain Michael Williams "said that the dead man's father, John D. O'Brien, told him that Manning had a gun when he came upstairs to invite his son down to his apartment. A short time after the two men went to Manning's apartment, the elder O'Brien was quoted by police as saying, he was on his way down to ask his son and Manning to tone down the phonograph when he heard two shots. Police found O'Brien slumped in a chair and Manning lying unconscious on the floor. Manning was taken to St. Anne's hospital where a police guard was placed at his bedside" (*Fitchburg Sentinel*).

THE TRIAL

A manslaughter charge was presented at trial by the prosecution.

OUTCOME

Manning was sentenced to three to five years in prison in solitary confinement.

FURTHER READING

"Fall River Man Slain by Friend." *Fitchburg Sentinel* (Fitchburg, Massachusetts), January 12, 1948.

"Nothing in Annals of Fall River Attracted As Much Attention as Borden Murder Case," *Fall River Herald News* (Fall River, Massachusetts), September 19, 1958.

GALLERY

John P. Manning, Jr.

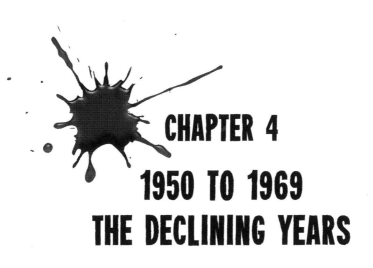

CHAPTER 4
1950 TO 1969
THE DECLINING YEARS

In the 1950s, the cities of the SouthCoast were in the midst of the great decline. Fall River and New Bedford's population dropped 3% and 1% from the decade before and would drop another 11% and 6% by 1960. Towns such as Somerset and Fairhaven grew at a record pace, increasing in 1950 by 45% and 17%. The American work force was seeing a tremendous shift from manufacturing to service. By 1956, a majority of Americans and SouthCoast workers were white-collar rather and blue-collar. The demand for single-family homes increased as the widespread ownership of automobiles enabled a great migration from the cities to the suburbs and beyond. And let's not discount the importance of the invention of air conditioning to the burgeoning markets in "Sun Belt" areas of the South and West—Florida, Texas, and Arizona, causing thousands of jobs to move away from New England.

Due to the loss of manufacturing jobs, particularly for men, an effort began to expand industrialization in the area. A new industrial park was created in the north end of the city of Fall River. Its objective was to create new, good-paying jobs for the heads of households. Unfortunately, for every good new job created a like number seemed to end as businesses closed or failed. On the job front, the SouthCoast was merely spinning its wheels.

Good things happened as well. Newly relocated professional Dr. Irving Fradkin created an organization called Citizens Scholarship Foundation, which morphed into a national movement to assist youngsters going on to higher education with financial aid that continues to this day. SouthCoast residents and tourists from around the globe flocked to the yearly Newport Jazz Festival where many future legends of the music world, like Ray Charles, BB King, and Stevie Wonder, would perform.

But let's not forget that the 1950s was also the advent of the drug era. And where there are drugs, unfortunately, there is also crime.

Murders became more frequent because of thefts and shootings. Cult members, child abusers, and police killers were snuffing out young people. Smaller, more quaint communities like Little Compton, Rhode Island, joined Tiverton, Rhode Island, and nearby Westport, Massachusetts, as locations where dastardly deeds were committed. Many of these murders remain unsolved to this day.

Many historic buildings were demolished in the two decades represented by this chapter. The heart of the city of Fall River, its grand City Hall, was torn down as Interstate 195 rushed up the gut of the city, sealing the fate of the mighty Quequechan River. Fall River was promised that by putting a highway through the middle of town, tourists would "naturally" flock to the city and partake of the night life, restaurants, and culture. Instead, the highway became a way for people to drive through, not drive to, Fall River as they rushed to Cape Cod and points south.

From its heyday in the 1920s to the 1940s, the SouthCoast had now become an afterthought—a place to move away from, and Fall River and New Bedford were on the brink of learning a most valuable lesson: the days of prosperity were behind them and the future did not look much brighter than it does today.

BARBARA, SANDRA, DIANE, AND BARRY GOLAS

CRIME
Man kills his entire family (wife and three children) and then commits suicide in their home at 2 Ocean Court, Fairhaven, Massachusetts, on April 6, 1950.

VICTIM
Barbara, 27, Sandra, 6, Diane, 5, Barry, 2, Golas

ACCUSED
Walter J. Golas, 31

DETAILS
An entire family of five was discovered dead in the gas-filled home on April 8, 1950. "The tragedy was discovered when police broken into the four-room cottage after a relative reported the mother had not been heard from since last Wednesday ... Mrs. Golas, police said, was lying face down on the divan, her skull apparently crushed by a blunt instrument. [Walter] Golas was on the floor beside a gas stove in an alcove used as a pantry. The older children were found in bed in one room, and two-year-old Barry was in a crib in another room. Police Chief Norman D. Shurtleff said there was nothing to indicated when or how the family died ... On the floor near Mrs. Golas' body was a four-inch piece of pipe, about an inch and a half in diameter. There was no blood on the pipe, Shurtleff said" (*Arizona Republic*).

The medical examiner determined that Mrs. Golas died Wednesday or Thursday and the other family members not long after.

The family "had been exposed to a large amount of escaping illuminating gas and the bodies of the parents appeared to have wounds from which blood had flowed" (*Long Beach Independent*). Authorities believed that all of the children had died from gas poisoning.

Medical Examiner William Rosen determined that Walter Golas had bludgeoned his wife to death and then "asphyxiated himself and his three children. Dr. Rosen gave a verdict of homicide and suicide after the autopsy on the body of Mrs. Golas" (*The Pantagraph*). Financial troubles, including an impending eviction, were blamed for the deaths.

The medical examiner said that he "was told by relatives of the family that the Golas house had been sold and the new owner had given an eviction notice. He said he learned also that Golas had worried lately over finances" (*Democrat and Chronicle*).

THE TRIAL

There was no trial as this was a murder/suicide.

AFTERWORD

Walter J. Golas, was honorably discharged from the army, with the rank of private, on September 3, 1943. The house where the tragedy took place has been torn down and is now an empty lot.

FURTHER READING

"Family of 5 Found Dead in House." *The Philadelphia Inquirer* (Philadelphia, Pennsylvania), April 9, 1950.
"Family of Five Dead in Murder, Suicide." *The Berkshire Eagle* (Pittsfield, Massachusetts), April 10, 1950.
"Father Kills Family, Self." *The Pantagraph* (Bloomington, Illinois), April 10, 1050.
"Find Parents, 3 Children Dead." *Long Beach Independent* (Long Beach, California), April 9, 1950.
"4 Killings, Suicide in Family Traced to Housing Worry." *Democrat and Chronicle* (Rochester, New York), April 10, 1950.
"Five Members of Family Found Dead in Home." *Hartford Courant* (Hartford, Connecticut), April 9, 1950.
"Tragedy Cause Fixed." *Newport Daily News* (Newport, Rhode Island), April 10, 1950.
"Whole Family of Five Wiped Out in Mystery." *Arizona Republic* (Phoenix, Arizona), April 9, 1950.

EINER V. ANDERSON

CRIME	Man kills his employer in argument over a dog at 37 Hedge Street, in Fairhaven, Massachusetts, on April 18, 1953.
VICTIM	Einer V. Anderson, 52
ACCUSED	Carl Frederick Berg, 65

DETAILS

Einer Anderson, a hotel janitor, of Bridgeport, Connecticut, was stabbed to death at a home he owned in Fairhaven, Massachusetts, by Carl Berg, the caretaker of the property.

"Police Chief Norman D. Shurtleff said Anderson was spending the week at his bungalow and that the two men got into an argument over Anderson's dog. Anderson was stabbed four times with a six-inch hunting knife. Police said they are holding a New Bedford woman, identified as Ruth Murray Delano, 35, as a material witness" (*Hartford Courant*). Anderson was taken to Acushnet Hospital but died of his wounds.

OUTCOME

Records or reports of the trial cannot be located.

FURTHER READING

"Bridgeport Man Dies of Stabbing Wounds." *Hartford Courant* (Hartford, Connecticut), April 19, 1953.

GALLERY

37 Hedge Street, Fairhaven, MA, as it stands today.

MARY DUARTE

CRIME

Man kills his wife and then self in their home in Fairhaven, Massachusetts, on September 13, 1953.

VICTIM

Mary Duarte, 38

ACCUSED

John Duarte, 47

DETAILS

John Duarte, an amateur song writer and formerly a violin and trumpet teacher, was distraught over the marriage of his eldest daughter, Philomena, 19, to Henry Grigorian, an assistant instructor at the Boston University School of Music and a concert pianist. He so opposed the marriage that he refused to attend the ceremony the day before at St. James Armenian Church in Watertown (another newspaper said that he was not invited).

Duarte thought that his daughter's marriage to Grigorian would mean she would have to give up her own music career as a violinist. John and Mary Duarte argued violently over the marriage, according to their youngest daughter, Gertrude, 13. After the two other children, Joanne, 9, and Philip, 3, went to an upstairs room, John Duarte shot and killed his wife and committed suicide with a 22-caliber repeater rifle. A son, John, 17, was not at home.

"After hearing two shots [Gertrude] rushed downstairs to find her mother sprawled in a bedroom and her father on the kitchen floor" (*The Baltimore Sun*).

John Duarte had published two songs, "I Have Done All I Can For You" and "Amore De Pai" (Love of Peace). He operated a 60-acre farm and was an unsuccessful candidate for the board of health in the election the year before.

THE TRIAL

There was no trial as this was a murder/suicide.

FURTHER READING

"Couple Slain After Nuptials of Daughter." *The Times* (Shreveport, Louisiana), September 14, 1953.

"Father of Five Kills Wife, Ends Own Life." *Hartford Courant* (Hartford, Connecticut), September 14, 1953.

"Girl's Marriage to Violinist Leads to Double Killing." *The Post-Standard* (Syracuse, New York), September 14, 1953.

"Kills Wife and Himself After Marriage Row." *Moberly Monitor-Index* (Moberly, Missouri), September 14, 1953.

"Kills Wife and Self After Daughter Weds." *Chicago Daily Tribune* (Chicago, Illinois), September 14, 1953.

"Musician Kills Wife, Self in Row Over Daughter's Career." *The Portsmouth Herald* (Portsmouth, New Hampshire), September 14, 1953.

"Song Writer, 47, Kills Wife, Self." *The Daily Courier* (Connellsville, Pennsylvania), September 14, 1953.

"Two Die in Rift Over Wedding of Daughter." *The Baltimore Sun* (Baltimore, Maryland), September 14, 1953.

EMILY UDY

CRIME	Elderly lady viciously beaten and stabbed at 713 Davol Street, in Fall River, Massachusetts, on April 13, 1960.
VICTIM	Emily Udy, 72
ACCUSED	Robert Cusick, 16

DETAILS

A newspaper left on the stoop outside the cottage of an elderly single lady who lived alone on Davol Street in Fall River was a sign to the paper carrier that something was amiss with Miss Emily Udy. The towhead rapped timidly on the door of the house but there was no response. He had been Miss Udy's newspaper boy for two years and knew that she read the paper every day, that she was extremely interested in what went on in the world around her. If she had not picked up yesterday's *Herald News*, there was something wrong.

Conferring with the oil station owner across the street, they both decided to phone the police.

Emily Udy was retried from the income tax division of the Massachusetts Department of Corporations and Taxations.

Patrolman Alfred Picard arrived and found the front door locked. He went around the outside, trying windows and peering in, hoping that he would find an innocent explanation as to her whereabouts. He had to force open a side window to gain access. He found nothing in the downstairs living room and bedroom, but when he turned on the lights in the kitchen, "he saw the sinister path of streaked reddish-brown leading to the door of the woodshed" (*Detective Cases*).

When he looked down the steps into the shed, he saw a form covered with burlap bags and a bloody sheet. As he pulled back the coverings, he realized that he had found the grisly remains of Miss Emily Udy.

Fingerprints left in the house at the murder scene and in the upstairs bathroom where the murderer gained access led police to a neighborhood youth, Bob Cusick, who lived near Udy's home. The lead detective, Theodore Kaegael, found a pair of bloody scissors at the scene, and blood on a picket fence and tines on a pitchfork in the shed. They had been plunged into the elderly lady's neck and heart in her kitchen before she was dragged into the shed that adjoined the kitchen. Her body was covered with a burlap bag and found in the out shed. After fingerprints revealed the potential murderer was the young boy who attended the Ruggles School for special education students, he was questioned for a second time by police and admitted he killed the woman whom he had often befriended.

"Police Capt. James D. Crosson said Mrs. Udy had several puncture wounds on her chest and was badly beaten on the head. Her body was covered with a burlap bag and rags. Crossin said the woman was fully clothed and there was no sign of a struggle. He also said that robbery did not seem to be the motive" (*Newport Daily News*). *Detective Cases* reported that the autopsy, performed by Harvard's Dr. George Katsas, found that "death had been caused by multiple lacerations about the face and upper body, any one of which could have killed the victim. She had also been cruelly bludgeoned as revealed by many fractures and injuries on the upper part of the body. The stab wounds penetrated the heart and lungs, and there was a skull fracture. The knife, fence picket and pitchfork were doubtlessly the death weapons. The victim had been slain sometime between 11 a.m. and 1 p.m. Wednesday, April 19th. She had not been sexually attacked."

"Police said the boy told them the stabbing occurred when he broke into Mrs. Udy's home seeking stamps to add to his collection. The woman discovered him and took up a fence picket to drive him away. When the boy wrenched the picket out of her hands, she seized the scissors. Police said the boy told them he took the scissors away from her and stabbed her with them ... She had apparently been struck down from the rear and stabbed several times. A pair of scissors, believed to be the weapon, was found in an empty coal stove in the kitchen" (*Newport Daily News*).

Cusick had a prior juvenile record for attacking a young girl.

THE TRIAL

After a hearing in District Court, Robert Cusick, was held without bail for the Grand Jury and charged with murder. He was confused and an innocent plea was entered for him. Robert, the son of Mr. and Mrs. Edward F. Cusick, was first arraigned as a juvenile and then brought into open court and arraigned as an adult. He was charged with first degree murder. Cusick was ruled to be insane.

OUTCOME

Robert Cusick was sentenced to the Bridgewater State Hospital. In 1965, at the age of 21, he was ruled as fit to stand trial for the 1960 saying of Miss Emily Udy. No other reporting on his case has been located.

FURTHER READING

Belton, H. H. "The House of Davol Street." *Detective Cases*, Volume 7, No. 2, August, 1906.
"Boy, 16, Held in Murder of Elderly Woman." *The Berkshire Eagle* (Pittsfield, Massachusetts), April 22, 1960.
"Cops Hold Boy in Stab-Slaying." *The Bridgeport Post* (Bridgeport, Connecticut), April 22, 1960.
"Fall River Boy Held in Slaying." *Newport Daily News* (Newport, Rhode Island), April 22, 1960.
"Fall River Slaying of Woman Probed." *Newport Daily News* (Newport, Rhode Island), April 15, 1960.

GALLERY

Mrs. Udy's shed, where her body was discovered. *Detective Cases*, 1960.

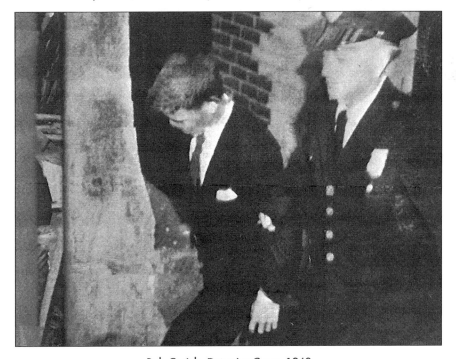

Bob Cusick. *Detective Cases*, 1960.

Newsboy James Hague, who first noticed something was amiss. *Detective Cases*, 1960.

Detective fitting the post to its missing space in Mrs. Udy's fence. *Detective Cases*, 1960.

HERBERT JOHN STRAKER, JR.

CRIME	Man shot during an argument about the ownership of a boat on the beach in Westport, Massachusetts, on June 10, 1961.
VICTIM	Herbert John Straker, Jr., 55
ACCUSED	John Baker, 51

DETAILS

On June 10, 1961, a group of four men, including Herbert Straker, went to Baker's Beach to discuss salvaging a stranded 48-foot sloop, *Dora*, that had washed ashore in heavy fog about 700 feet to the west of Baker's property. Note: Baker's Beach was named after the owner, John Baker, and still called this to this day.

Straker was interested in the boat and, while Baker was at home, drove his wife and two large Weimaraner dogs to the beach entrance where he was met by a special police officer of the town, named Duffy. The officer thought that Straker was not a member but the wife assured him that she was. Duffy told Straker that he would let Baker know he was again violating rules and that Baker would return their membership check and that their membership would end.

Straker drove to a nearby inn and began drinking vodka. Accompanied by a member of the beach club, Straker returned with his dogs, driving at a "very high rate of speed" (forty to forty-five miles per hour). Duffy had to jump back to avoid being run over. Straker parked the car in an unauthorized place and spent a quarter of an hour on the beach, then returned to the inn.

It was here that Straker picked up Harney, Lees, and Reed, drove them back to the beach to see the sloop. By this time Baker had arrived and was being informed about Straker's behavior by Duffy. Straker drove in at an even faster rate of speed than before and didn't stop or slow. Each member of the group had a different memory of this part of the story, with Reed saying they did not stop, Lees saying they came "almost to a stop," and Harney saying they had to stop because there were two cars in the driveway.

As they sped past Baker, they yelled something at him. Baker investigated the parked car and saw the dogs, realizing that the man was the same "troublemaker" that he had encountered before. Baker went to the pump house and retrieved his gun, figuring, he said, that the gang of men would be less likely to attack him if he had a weapon.

Baker, as owner of the property, blew a whistle, and ordered the men to leave, firing a warning shot into the sand. A very heated argument occurred and "harsh words were exchanged." According to witnesses, Straker struck first, punching Baker in the face, an act that knocked his glasses off his face. Baker then fired two bullets at point range into Straker, killing him instantly.

This was not the first time the two men had quarreled. Baker had also been increasingly upset that Straker allowed his dogs to run free on the beach, against posted rules, parked a number of times in an unauthorized place, and, on two occasions, had driven rapidly and unsafely at the beach club owned and operated by Baker.

"Dr. Arthur LaSalle, medical examiner, said Straker died instantly, death resulting from two .32 caliber revolver rounds fired at close range. One of the bullets struck Straker in the chest and severed the pulmonary artery. Dr. LaSalle reported this caused a massive hemorrhage resulting in instantaneous death. The second bullet glanced off the victim's wrist and entered the abdomen. Police said a warning shot into a sand dune had also been fired. The body was face down in the sand some 200 feet from the grounded vessel when they arrived, police said" (*Fall River Herald News*).

John H. Baker lived at 1097 Drift Road in Westport, Massachusetts.

Straker was survived by a wife, sister, mother, two daughters, and two grandchildren.

THE TRIAL

Baker entered a plea of innocent and claimed self-defense. Harney testified that he saw the punch, while

Reed heard no whistles. Reed said he heard the warning shot and, turning, saw Baker running down the beach to them. Reed witnessed Straker making a swinging motion and Baker's glasses fall. Lees heard the "pop" of the gun and continued toward the sloop. He then heard another shot, turned, and saw Baker fire the second shot at Straker.

The court found that Baker had executed "extraordinarily bad judgment to procure a loaded revolver as a means of enforcing the regulations, and it was an unfortunate act to fire it into the sand as a means of attracting attention."

The jury convicted him of first degree murder.

OUTCOME

Baker was sentenced to life in prison. Baker was the first person in Massachusetts history to be free on bail while awaiting trial for murder.

AFTERWORD

In 1963, on appeal to a three-judge court, the charge was reduced to manslaughter and a 2-½ year sentence was imposed. Baker was paroled after serving only fourteen months in jail, and pardoned in 1970. Local opinion was divided with some believing that Baker got away with murder. Others, who were his friends before the shooting, stood by him. John Baker eventually sold all his property and moved to Arizona.

FURTHER READING

"Baker Enters Plea Of Innocent to Murder Charge." *Fall River Herald News* (Fall River, Massachusetts), June 12, 1961.

"Commonwealth vs. John H. Baker." Justia US Law. law.justia.com/cases/massachusetts/supreme-court/volumes/346/346mass107.html

GALLERY

John Baker.

RUTH M. FULLER

CRIME Woman strangled to death in her apartment at 53 Reynolds Street, in Fairhaven, Massachusetts, on June 30, 1962.

VICTIM Ruth M. Fuller, 40

ACCUSED Jackie Lee Wood, 19

DETAILS Jackie Lee Wood, of Little Rock, Arkansas, a sailor aboard the destroyer *Willard Keith*, was in New Bedford for the July 4 celebration. It was while in that city that he met waitress Ruth M. Fuller. He paid a visit to her in her apartment in Fairhaven and, when she spurned his advances, strangled her.

Wood was indicted for murder in the second degree.

THE TRIAL There was evidence placing Wood at the scene of the crime, including the fact that he left his wallet in her bedroom where the body was found. But there were no witnesses or direct evidence to prove he was the killer.

OUTCOME After deliberating two hours and fifteen minutes, Jackie Lee Wood was acquitted of a murder in the second degree on March 21, 1963.

AFTERWORD The worst possible thing happened following Jackie Lee Wood's acquittal for the strangulation death of Ruth M. Fuller—he killed again.

Wood returned to his home of Arkansas and on September 15, 1964, strangled and killed 17-year-old Pamela Ann King of Little Rock. Her naked body was found in a downtown Little Rock motel room. Police Chief R.E. Brains said that the fingerprints found at the scene of the crime matched those of Jackie Lee Wood and the room where the body was discovered was registered to Wood. He was arrested a short time after the killing of King.

Pamela Ann King had been sexually molested.

Wood pleaded innocent to the charge by reason of insanity. After conducting tests, the State Hospital reported that Wood was without psychosis and could stand trial, which was scheduled for early December. He was charged with first degree murder.

During the trial, Wood changed his plea to innocent. Wood took the stand in his own defense, saying that he had met Pamela Ann King at a private club, danced with her, and she agreed to go to the motel with him. He said she changed her mind before they arrived and they parted company on Main Street. He then went to two restaurants and the bus station. When he returned to the hotel room, he said he found the girl dead. He claimed he had told her the room number before they parted ways earlier in the evening.

On December 5, 1964, after deliberating for two hours, the jury found Wood guilty and recommended a life sentence.

While serving that life sentence, Wood, now 25, and two other prisoners escaped from the Tucker Prison Farm in Tucker, Arkansas in May of 1967. Wood was described as five feet, 10 inches tall, weighing 175 pounds, and having brown hair and hazel eyes. He also had several tattoo marks on his arms. The three had broken into a clothes locker at the prison and put on street clothes. The fugitives were considered armed and dangerous.

All three were captured after a gun fight, with one of the escapees, William Moore, 23, dying of his head injuries. Wood was wounded in the shoulder and returned to Tucker.

Apparently, the prison where Wood was sent to had quite a reputation as an easy place to escape from because trusty inmates guarded other prisoners. Between January 1 and mid-May, twenty-seven inmates had escaped from Tucker.

In a final twist to the story of Jackie Lee Wood, Governor Frank White granted him parole in 1982 at the age of 39. The mother of murder victim Pamela Ann

King said she learned from newspapers that White had commuted King's sentence and he had not informed her. The Governor apologized to the distraught mother, saying they could not locate her to inform her of the state's decision.

"'He said, "Mrs. King, I can sympathize." And I said, 'No, Governor White, you cannot sympathize with me. When that man puts his bare hands around your daughter's neck, then you can sympathize with me,' she said" (*The Times*).

FURTHER READING

"Captured Convict Dies From Wounds." *Northwest Arkansas Times* (Fayetteville, Arkansas), May 25, 1967.

"Charge Filed in Strangulation." *Northwest Arkansas Times* (Fayetteville, Arkansas), September 17, 1964.

"Escape Ends Interview at Prison." *Fairbanks Daily News-Miner* (Fairbanks, Alaska), May 20, 1967.

"Girl Had Been Sexually Molested." *Hope Star* (Hope, Arkansas), September 25, 1964.

"Governor Apologizes." *The Times* (Shreveport, Louisiana), January 14, 1982.

"Guilty Verdict Returned in Murder Case." *The Times* (Shreveport, Louisiana), December 6, 1964.

"Indicted for Murder." *Lansing State Journal* (Lansing, Michigan), November 15, 1962.

The Irving Daily News Texan (Irving, Texas), September 17, 1964.

"Little Rock." *The El Dorado Times* (El Dorado, Arkansas), October 23, 1964.

"Motions Overruled in Murder Case." *Northwest Arkansas Times* (Fayetteville, Arkansas), December 1, 1964.

"Murder Trial Set." *Northwest Arkansas Times* (Fayetteville, Arkansas), November 2, 1964.

"Navy Man Acquitted in Woman's Slaying." *Newport Daily News* (Newport, Rhode Island), March 23, 1963.

"News Conference the 'Time' For Escape, Prisoner Felt." *The Cincinnati Enquirer* (Cincinnati, Ohio), May 21, 1967.

"Police on Alert for 3 Escapees." *Longview News-Journal* (Longview, Texas), May 19, 1967.

"Sailor, 19, Acquitted in Death of Woman, 40." *The North Adams Transcript* (North Adams, Massachusetts), March 22, 1963.

"State Rests Case Against Jack Wood." *Northwest Arkansas Times* (Fayetteville, Arkansas), December 5, 1964.

"Three Tucker Inmates are Recaptured." *El Dorado Daly News* (El Dorado, Arkansas), May 21, 1967,

"Wounded Tucker Escapee Said in 'Bad Shape.'" *Northwest Arkansas Times* (Fayetteville, Arkansas), May 22, 1967.

GALLERY

Pamela Ann King. *The Irving Daily News Texan*, September 17, 1964.

JEAN THIBEAULT

CRIME	Robbery and murder at the Borden Street café in Fall River, Massachusetts, late one night in 1963.
VICTIM	Jean Thibeault, 45
ACCUSED	John Petetabella, 19, Joseph Robideau, 21, and Gerald Sousa, 21.

DETAILS

Mr. Jean Thibeault owned Padden's Café. John Petetabella, Gerald Sousa, and Joseph Robideau entered the cafe with the plan of robbing it.

According to court records, "About 1 A.M. December 28, 1963, three men entered Padden's Cafe in Fall River. There were already five people in the establishment, including the proprietor, Jean Thibeault, an employee, Albert Brulotte, and a customer, Barbara Ferree. The newcomers asked for beer and were advised that the bar was closed. They then requested change for cigarettes and were told that the cash had been put away. They next sought the use of the 'men's room' and two of them entered it singly, the second returning with a stocking mask over his face and carrying a gun.

"There was testimony that this was the defendant Gerald Sousa. One of his companions, one Petetabella, then announced, 'This is a stickup,' and ordered Thibeault and Brulotte to go into the kitchen and lie on the floor face down. The third intruder, Joseph Robideau, commanded Barbara Ferree 'to get down' and held a knife to her abdomen.

"Several shots were then fired by one of the men in the kitchen. One of the shots hit Thibeault in the right chest causing his death. In addition, he sustained two head wounds which a medical witness ascribed to blunt force injury. Another shot grazed the right shoulder of Brulotte sufficiently close to leave a hole in the sweater which he was wearing. Brulotte's wallet was then extracted from his left hip pocket. After the shots the three left the establishment. As they left, Barbara Ferree's wallet was taken by one of the men; in the process she was clubbed on the head and left with injuries requiring a week's hospitalization.

"[Sousa] was indicted for the murder of Thibeault in company with Petetabella and Robideau, as well as for armed robbery while masked of Thibeault, Brulotte, and Ferree, and assault and battery with a dangerous weapon on Ferree. He was convicted on all of these indictments. Since the jury made a recommendation that the death sentence be not imposed on the murder charge, [Sousa] was sentenced to life imprisonment. Sentences for terms of years to be served concurrently with his life sentence were imposed for the other crimes of which he was convicted. In addition to the three principals, all of whom received life terms, Manuel Aguiar and two other individuals, who took part in conferences with the principals before and after the crimes for which they were convicted, were charged as accessories."

THE TRIAL

According to testimony, "Thibeault was killed after Petetabella and Joseph Robideau went to Fall River to attend a bachelor party for their friend Gerald Sousa. After drinking heavily, Petetabella and Robideau robbed three workers at a market. Petetabella pistol-whipped a worker so severely that he broke the trigger guard of his pistol.

"After the robbery, Petetabella suggested they go to a bar because on a Friday night, a bar would be full of customers with money. The three men arrived at Padden's Café, where Petetabella, armed with a gun, ordered Thibeault and a bar employee to lie face down on the kitchen floor. Petetabella and Sousa took their wallets. When Thibeault reached up toward Petetabella, he shot him once through the back" (*Fall River Herald News*).

Petetabella admitted he shot the victim in the back, claiming he was drunk and insane. He was spared the death penalty. All three defendants were convicted of first-degree murder and sentenced to life in prison. Gerald Sousa provided the police with a full confession.

OUTCOME

The jury sentenced Petetabella to life in prison for first degree murder, sparing them all the death penalty. Massachusetts has not executed anyone since 1947 and abolished the death penalty in 1984. Each of the convicted men also were sentenced to concurrent terms of 15 to 25 years and 5 to 10 years on armed robbery and assault charges.

Forty-four years later, a motion for a new trial was denied by the Superior Court.

AFTERWORD

Gerald J. Sousa was arrested ninety minutes after he was married, at his wedding reception, by a squad of eight police officers. The bride, her parents, and guests had no idea what was happening or that Sousa was involved in any crime. Sousa had a record, however, appearing in court in Newport on several occasions, once for carrying a pistol without a permit. He was sentenced to six months in the Adult Correctional Institution in Rhode Island. He also had an assault charge.

At the time of this murder, Petetabella's father, Joseph, was serving a life prison term in Connecticut for the 1952 hitchhike slaying of George Zgierski of Hartford, Connecticut. Joseph was 37 when he and William J. Lorain, 33, killed the Polish man. Zgierski had offered the two men a ride in his car. His body was found a few days later. Lorrain died in the electric chair on July 11, 1955. Petetabella turned state's evidence and was given life, after pleading guilty to second degree murder. Joseph's wife also had a police record when, in 1946, she and her husband and Mrs. Ernestine Hutton, were accused of throwing a towel-wrapped gun into the Rhode Island State Prison, intended for Mrs. Hutton's husband. Mrs. Petetabella was given a deferred sentence and her husband, Joseph, was given seven years in prison. It was upon his release that he murdered Mr. Zgierski.

FURTHER READING

"Bay State Cafe Owner Shot, Killed in Holdup." *Hartford Courant* (Hartford, Connecticut), December 29, 1963.
"Commonwealth vs. Gerald Sousa." Justia US Law. law.justia.com/cases/massachusetts/supreme-court/volumes/350/350mass591.html
"Groom Held in Cafe Slaying." *Nashua Telegraph* (Nashua, New Hampshire), December 30, 1963.

"Life for Trio in Fall River Slay Holdup." *Nashua Telegraph* (Nashua, New Hampshire), July 6, 1964.

"Man Loses Bid for New Trial in 1963 Murder." *Fall River Herald News* (Fall River, Massachusetts), March 31, 2011.

"Newlywed Arrested in Slaying." *Hartford Courant* (Hartford, Connecticut), December 30, 1963.

"Slain Man Navy Worker; Suspect Has Record Here." *Newport Mercury* (Newport, Rhode Island), January 3, 1964.

"Three Plead Innocent in Bay State Shooting." *Nashua Telegraph* (Nashua, New Hampshire), January 4, 1964.

ANNE C. BROWNELL

CRIME	Woman beaten to death with a rock on Warren Point Road in Little Compton, Rhode Island, on April 21, 1965.
VICTIM	Anne C. Brownell, 18
ACCUSED	Stanley Gendreau, 22
DETAILS	Stanley Gendreau, the son of a housekeeper in Little Compton, Rhode Island, smashed the teenage victim in the head with a rock and killed her in 1965.

The body of Anne Brownell was found at 2 a.m. in a brush-grown area behind two vacant homes, 200 yards away from the home of Republican Rhode Island State Senator Maxwell C. Huntoon. She had been babysitting for three of his grandchildren when she was murdered. When the Senator and his wife returned home, they found her missing and called the police.

Police said that they discovered a large pool of blood on the road in front of the Senator's home. While they did not know how or why she was outside, it appeared that she was attacked at that location. "Police followed a trail of blood from the point on the road to about 75 yards behind two vacant summer cottages and into a thicket, where the body was found" (*Newport News*).

A 40-year-old man was questioned and then released after passing a lie detector test.

Said the local police, "A number of things have been forwarded to the FBI laboratory in Washington, including two stones believed to be the murder weapons, a blood-stained sailcloth clothes bag and strands of hair found on Warren Point Road where the initial assault is thought to have occurred" (*Biddeford-Saco Journal*).

The chief medical examiner attributed the cause of death to multiple skull fractures. Brownell was fully-clothed when found but they are not ruling out that she was sexually molested until tests are completed.

Police reported that Brownell had been talking with her boyfriend on the phone from 7 to 8 p.m. A female motorist who happened by the house about 9 p.m. observed the pool of blood in the road and thought an animal had been hit by a car.

Police soon arrested Stanley Gendreau, 22, of Little Compton, a carpenter, for the murder. His mother, Mrs. Stanley J. Gendreau, was employed as a domestic at the Huntoon home. He had learned from his mother that Anne Brownell was babysitting that night.

The grand jury returned a true bill and charged Stanley Gendreau with the murder of Anne Brownell. He pleaded innocent. He was then sent to the Adult Correctional Institution at Cranston, to be held without bail, until his trial for first degree murder.

In June, 1965, a mental test was ordered by the Attorney General, stating that a psychiatrist should be appointed to determine if Gendreau is mentally capable of standing trial. On December 31, 1964, Stanley Gendreau had received a medial discharge from the Navy because he was suffering from a personality disorder of a schizoid type.

Gendreau's lawyer left the case before the trial started, necessitating a new lawyer being brought on and up to speed. Because of this development, the trial was postponed. The defense then argued that the press coverage was such that a fair trial could not be had in Newport. The judge agreed to a change of venue to Providence County.

THE TRIAL

A psychiatrist testified that Gendreau was "criminally insane" at the time of the murder, but the Superior Court judge ordered the testimony to be disregarded.

The trial began on October 3, 1966, and concluded on November 25, 1966. After almost eleven hours of deliberation, the jury found Gendreau guilty of murder in the second degree.

OUTCOME

Stanley Gendreau was sentenced to life in prison. Superior Court Judge Joseph R. Weisberger said that it was necessary to send him away for life "to protect both society and the defendant from the consequences of his action."

AFTERWORD

In 1970, Gendreau was granted a new trial because his defense argued, and the Supreme Court of Rhode Island agreed, that the defendant had not been read his Miranda rights at the time of his arrest, making his statements to the police inadmissible. In 1978, Gendreau lived in Cranston, Rhode Island. He was paroled in 1980 under the condition that he never again returns to the town of Little Compton, Rhode Island. His parents continued to live in Little Compton until his father died in 1978 of natural causes.

FURTHER READING

"Baby-Sitter, 18, Slain; Body Found in Woods." *Newport Daily News* (Newport, Rhode Island), April 22, 1965.
"Gendreau Given Life for Murder of Girl." *Newport Daily News* (Newport, Rhode Island), January 19, 1967.
"Girl, 18, Is Slain in R.I." *Fitchburg Sentinel* (Fitchburg, Massachusetts), April 22, 1965.
"Jury Calls Witnesses in Slaying." *Newport Daily News* (Newport, Rhode Island), April 30, 1965.
"Jury Convicts Man of Murder." *Hartford Courant* (Hartford, Connecticut), November 27, 1966.
"Jury Hears Testimony From Blood Specialist." *Newport Daily News* (Newport, Rhode Island), October 26, 1966.
"Man Convicted of Murder Will be Given New Trial." *Newport Daily News* (Newport, Rhode Island), December 12, 1969.
"Man, 22, Is Held for Slaying Girl." *Newport Daily News* (Newport, Rhode Island), April 24, 1965.
"Murder Trial Site Changed." *Newport Daily News* (Newport, Rhode Island), September 24, 1966.
"Police Continue Investigation of Girl's Murder." *Biddeford-Saco Journal* (Biddeford, Maine), April 23, 1965.
"Psychiatrist's Testimony Stricken in Gendreau Trial." *Newport Daily News* (Newport, Rhode Island), November 19, 1966.
"State Seeks Mental Test of Gendreau." *Newport Daily News* (Newport, Rhode Island), June 10, 1965.
"State v. Gendreau." Justia US Law. http://law.justia.com/cases/rhode-island/supreme-court/1969/259-a-2d-855-0.html
"Suspect Submits to Test, Is Freed." *Newport Daily News* (Newport, Rhode Island), April 23, 1965.

GALLERY

Ann C. Brownell. *Newport Daily News*, April 22, 1965.

CARL O. NAYLOR

CRIME

Gas station attendant was robbed, shot, and killed in Fall River, Massachusetts, on February 3, 1968.

VICTIM

Carl O. Naylor, 23

ACCUSED

Ronald Barboza, 20

DETAILS

Carl Naylor was an attendant during a robbery at the Mutual Gas Station on Broadway near South (Kennedy) Park near the site of the murder in 1832 of Sarah Maria Cornell. He closed up the station, secured the night's receipts, and unlocked the office door for the accused who killed him for the stations' and his money, netting $315.

At his arraignment, Ronald Barboza was adjudged probably guilty of murder and armed robbery. He was ordered held without bail for a grand jury. The grand jury indicted Barboza with first degree murder.

Barboza was the father of three children. Naylor was married to Eileen Aguiar Naylor and left behind two small children.

THE TRIAL

At his trial in October, Ronald Barboza pleaded guilty to a lesser charge second degree murder.

OUTCOME

Ronald Barboza was sentenced to a mandatory life prison term for the murder of Carl Naylor and given a concurrent twenty to thirty year prison term for the armed robbery. Barboza escaped from jail in 1975 but was recaptured and incarcerated again.

FURTHER READING

"Carl Naylor Rites." *Newport Daily News* (Newport, Rhode Island), February 7, 1968.

"Ex-McKinney Resident Shot to Death in Rhode Island Holdup." *The Advocate-Messenger* (Danville, Kennedy), February 8, 1968.

"Father of 3 Draws Life in Slaying." *Nashua Telegraph* (Nashua, New Hampshire), October 22, 1968.

"Man Arraigned in Murder Case." *Newport Daily News* (Newport, Rhode Island), February 27, 1968.

RUSSELL "RUSSGOLD" GOLDSTEIN

CRIME

Russell Goldstein was shot in his apartment above his antique store, RussGold Sporting Goods, at 420 South Main Street, corner of Morgan Street, in Fall River, Massachusetts, on December 20, 1969. This was a second attempt to kill Goldstein, a gun, antiques, and coin dealer.

VICTIM

Russell 'Russgold" Goldstein, 44

ACCUSED

Unsolved

DETAILS

Russell Goldstein was known to always to carry large sums of cash on his person and to like ladies of the night. The killer had easy access to his apartment above his store. In fact, there was no sign of forced entry which some say suggests he knew his assailant(s). It was rumored at the time that it may have been a mob killing because Goldstein was believed to be fencing stolen goods and dealing guns. The previous May, an attempt had been made on Goldstein's life.

In the encounter that ended his life, Russell Goldstein was shot four times with two different caliber guns. Three shots from a .22 in the chest, ear, and tight, and one shot in the hand from a .45. Goldstein had also been bludgeoned in the head, but it was unknown if this occurred before or after death. According the *Fall River Herald News* (December 22, 1969), "In the weeks [prior to] his death [but after the first attempt on Goldstein's life], three young men would die in Fall River. One died in a car crash [Frank Cabral, October 5]. Another hung himself in his own backyard, with his wrists handcuffed behind him [Normand Tremblay, October 14]. A third was found hanging in a police station holding cell [Thomas Collins, July 19]. Police involvement in the crimes was never proven. According to local rumor mongers, the three young men had been involved in a burglary ring that sold its spoils to Goldstein."

Suspicion fell on Sgt. Paul Gonsalves of the Fall River Police Department, who, it was discovered, ran a gang of burglars and allegedly fenced much of these stolen goods through Goldstein. The Sergeant was later convicted of extortion and kiting checks and served time in prison for those offenses.

Goldstein had been under investigation by the U.S. Treasury and the ATF was only days away with charging him for unreported buying and selling of weapons.

AFTERWORD

Author Joyce Keller Walsh has an interesting theory as to the culprit of the murder. After researching the case for a number of years, her book, *SLEUTH-blog*, offers a thoughtful analysis that is well worth reading.

FURTHER READING

"Agents Probe Goldstein Arsenal." *Fall River Herald News* (Fall River, Massachusetts), December 23, 1969.

Dion, Marc Munroe. "Lakeville Author Give Old, Unsolved Fall River Murder Case a New Set of Eyes." wickedlocal.com/x1402243893/Lakeville-author-gives-old-unsolved-Fall-River-murder-case-a-new-set-of-eyes

Moniz, William A. "Author Looks into Unsolved 1969 Killing." Southcoasttoday.com.

"Police Theorize Goldstein Knew Murderers." *Fall River Herald News* (Fall River, Massachusetts), December 22, 1969.

Walsh, Joyce Keller. *SLEUTH-blog: The Actual Investigation of a Cold-Case Murder*. Whiskey Creek Press, 2016.

GALLERY

Russell Goldstein with items he purchased in an auction in 1957. *Fall River Herald News.*

Russell Goldstein. *Fall River Herald News.*

ACKNOWLEDGMENTS & RESOURCES

As well as those below who have assisted in this effort, special thanks goes to Mary Faria, the librarian at *The Fall River Herald News*. She spent countless hours assisting me in finding news stories and photos to be reprinted from the archives. I would often leave the newsroom and say goodbye but she knew better and would offer a "see you soon." I would return in a few days with an "I'm back!" We communicated in person and frequently by email. I was in the newsroom so often they wanted to give me my own desk. Thanks, Mary, I could not have done it without you.

I also want to extend my appreciation to my new friend, Doreen Allen, a clerk in the Bristol County Superior Court Clerk's Office. Occasionally, news stories would provide me with the final disposition to the case but often they didn't and this necessitated a visit with Doreen in the Justice Center, second floor on South Main Street, in Fall River. Her associates would alert her to my presence with, "Doreen, your man is here."

She would then join me in a conference room and provide me with the trial dockets so that I could discover the results. We engaged in this activity frequently and she educated me to legal lingo and provided me with court documents to search. Doreen, I will miss our exchanges. Thanks for your help and smiles.

My trips to The Peoples University—the Fall River Public Library—were so frequent that the staff and other visitors to the Ryan Reference Room became friends. Special thanks to Dan Sheahan, who not only helped me gather information but supported my efforts with a friendly salutation—and machine operating instructions. Dan, we will see each other often in Westport if not Fall River.

When it came to asking the appropriate person to write the Foreword tot his book, Federal Judge Edward F. Harrington was on the top of the list. He has spent a half-century adjudicating criminal and civil cases. The retired judge still travels almost daily to his office in Boston to review and issue findings. Yet, he graciously found time to read over this tome and make remarks. He is true gentleman—the country, and especially this author, are lucky to have him. Thanks, Judge, for this effort—but, more importantly, your friendship.

Always helpful were Fall River historians Michael Martins and Dennis Binette, whose sources of information and fountains of knowledge are seemingly endless. Without these two gents, I could never have even started this investigation. A extra special thanks to Dennis, who after a busy season, also willingly agreed to write a sterling back page blurb for this book.

Special Thanks also to Attorney and Deputy District Attorney in Bristol County, William McCauley. McCauley, like the author, is a graduate of Portsmouth Priory and they both were taught English by the late Dom Damian Kearney, O.S.B. His days have been spent in court, filing charges and serving as the primary trial lawyer against many of those in future volumes of the book. His comments are most appreciated.

Cathe Moniz spent most of her life fighting crime from a position of authority in the Fall River Police Department. She knew murder first hand. Cathe was kind enough to sample this book and devote her time in retirement to verifying its accuracy. The time and insight she spent with me will shine forward into Volume Two, and her help has been truly inspirational. Thanks Deputy Chief.

Last, but certainly not least, it has been my good fortune to work with Stefani Koorey on a number of projects. This book could not have been possible without the amazing writing and research talents of co-author Stefani Koorey. From the first time a few years ago when I told her of my plans her eyes exploded and her excitement motivated me onward. This book is as much a part of her dedication as it is mine. Her editing and suggestions for changes to the text is par excellence and her creativity is fantastic. I am lucky that she still has time to edit my work (it truly needs it) and pass along needed suggestions and improvements to make the narrative and sequence read smoothly. Stef is another person who is a tremendous inspiration and benefit to our area and its history. Stick around, Stef.

Organizations:

SouthCoast Today
The Fall River Herald News
The Boston Globe
Fall River Historical Society—Michael Martins and Dennis Binette
Fall River Public Library—research staff
Staff at Notre Dame Cemetery
Marjory Gomez O'Toole, Managing Director, Little Compton Historical Society
Christine Miguel, Senior Records Clerk, Tiverton Police Department
Doreen G. Allen, Clerk, Bristol County Superior Court
Little Compton Police Department
Robin Perry, Bristol County Law Librarian
Hilary Kraus, UMass Dartmouth Librarian
Kathy Maiato, Asst. Somerset Town Clerk
(Ret.) Tom Eaton, Oak Grove Cemetery
Colin Furze, *Fall River Herald News*
State Library of Massachusetts

New Bedford Public Library
Dartmouth Public Library
Fairhaven Public Library
Ancestry.com
Newspapers.com

Published Sources:

Belton, H.H. "The House on Davol Street." *Detective Cases*, Vol. 7 # 2, August 1960.

Brayton, Alice. *Life on the Stream, Vol. 1*. Newport, RI: Wilkinson Press, 1962.

Brayton. Alice. *Life on the Stream, Vol. 2*. Newport, RI: Wilkinson Press, 1962.

Chapman, Sherry. *Lizzie Borden: Resurrections: A History of the People Surrounding the Borden Case Before, During, and After the Trial*. PearTree Press, 2014.

Commonwealth of Massachusetts VS. Lizzie A. Borden; The Knowlton Papers, 1892-1893. Eds. Michael Martins and Dennis A. Binette. Fall River, MA: Fall River Historical Society, 1994.

Conforti, Joseph A. *Lizzie Borden on Trial: Murder, Ethnicity, and Gender*. Kansas: University Press of Kansas, 2016.

Geary, Rick. *The Borden Tragedy*. New York: NBM Publishing, 1997.

Kasserman, David Richard. *Fall River Outrage: Life, Murder, and Justice in Early Industrial New England*. Philadelphia: University of Pennsylvania Press, 1986.

King, Irving H. *The Coast Guard Expands, 1865 - 1915: New Roles, New Frontiers*. Annapolis, MD: Naval Institute Press, 1996.

Lisle, Janet. *The History of Little Compton, A Home By the Sea, 1820-1950*. Little Compton: Little Compton Historical Society, 2012.

LizzieAndrewBorden.com

Martins, Michael & Binette, Dennis A. *Parallel Lives: A Social History of Lizzie Borden and Her Fall River*. Fall River: Fall River Historical Society, 2010.

Miller, Sarah. *The Borden Murders: Lizzie Borden and the Trial of the Century*. New York: Schwartz & Wade, 2016.

MurderByGaslight.com

Officer Down Memorial Page

Pearson, Edmund. *The Trial of Lizzie Borden*. New York: Doubleday, 1937. Rpt. as The Trial of Lizzie Borden by Edmund Pearson; Notable Trials Library Edition, Foreword by Alan Dershowitz. Delran, NJ: Gryphon, 1991.

Phillips, Arthur Sherman. *The Phillips History of Fall River, Fascicle I*. Fall River: Dover Press, 1944.

Phillips, Arthur Sherman. *The Phillips History of Fall River, Fascicle II*. Fall River: Dover Press, 1945.

Phillips, Arthur Sherman. *The Phillips History of Fall River, Fascicle III*. Fall River: Dover Press, 1946.

Porter, Edwin H. *The Fall River Tragedy*. Fall River, MA: George R. H. Buffinton, Press of J. D. Munroe, 1893. Rpt. with new introduction by Robert Flynn. Portland, ME: King Philip Pub., 1985.

Radin, Edward D. *Lizzie Borden: The Untold Story*. NY: Simon and Schuster, 1961.

Raven, Rory. *Wicked Conduct: The Minister, The Mill Girl, and the Murder that Captivated Old Rhode Island*. SC: History Press, 2009.

Rebello, Leonard. *Lizzie Borden: Past and Present*. Al-Zach Press, 1999.

Walsh, Joyce Keller. *SLEUTH-blog*. Whiskey Creek Press, 2016.

Williams, Catherine Read. *Fall River: An Authentic Narrative*. Boston: Lilly, Wait & Col, 1834.

Unpublished Sources:

Detective Cases, 1960
Scrapbook clippings of James F. O'Brien, Esq., 1911-1923

Individuals:

Kathryn Casey
Debbie Charpentier
Thomas Coughlin
(Ret.) Correctional Officer Russell Curran
Atty. Richard Desjardins
Jonathan Eaker
Barry French
Ransom Griffin
(Ret.) F.B.I. Agent Robert Hargraves
Mrs. Barbara Hayes
(Ret.) Det. Theodore Kaegael
Mary Ellen Kennedy
(Ret.) Judge Joseph I. Macy, Esq.
(Ret.) Deputy Chief of Police Fall River, Cathe Moniz
(Ret.) Fall River Chief of Police Daniel Racine
Cukie Macomber
Atty. Peter Paull
Daniel Sheahan
Dr. Philip Silvia
Thomas Slaight
Somerset Police

INDEX

by Stefani Koorey, PhD

Entries are arranged in letter-by-letter order, using the *Chicago Manual of Style, 16th Edition*. References to page numbers for illustrations are indicated by numerals in bold type.

NOTES

NOTES

ABOUT THE AUTHOR

John B. Cummings, Jr. is a life-long resident of Greater Fall River. His roots go deep, as his grandfather was a Fall River Mayor and his father a practicing attorney in the area for over fifty years.

The author spent his early career years as a bank vice president in the marketing department. He was recognized with advertising copy writing awards for many years. He than became the chief professional officer of the United Way of Greater Fall River where, among other tasks, he authored press releases, wrote promotional material, and annual reports. He retired from the United Way as Endowment Director and was recognized nationally for the program's success. In 2005, he wrote his first historical book for private consumption about the history of the Greater Fall River Development Corporation: *From Little Acorns to Giant Oaks*.

In 2011, the author continued writing local historical books; *The Last Fling-Hurricane Carol 1954*; *Cream of the Crop: Fall River's Best and Brightest*; and most recently *Lobstah Tales: the history of the Moby Dick/Back Eddy Restaurant in Westport, Massachusetts*. He also produced a *Last Fling* DVD with actual hurricane footage and survivor interviews. All books and the DVD are available through the publisher's web site: HillsideMedia.net

This current venture took two years to research and write and includes well over 250 solved and still mysterious murders, manslaughters, and mayhem in the eight SouthCoast cities and towns around Greater Fall River. His extensive research was conducted in the Fall River Public Library, The *Fall River Herald News* Library, and the clerk's office of the Bristol County Superior Court, as well as on the Internet.

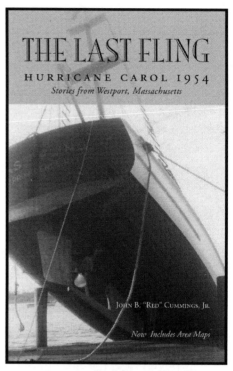

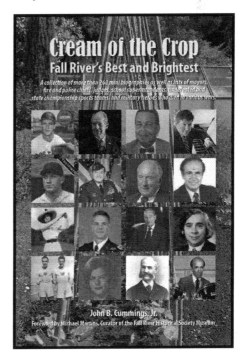

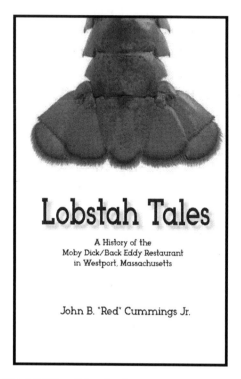

47270204R00137

Made in the USA
Middletown, DE
20 August 2017